W9-ARN-327

Everybody

Eats

■ ■ ■

Everybody Eats

*supermarket consumers
in the 1990s*

Marcia Mogelonsky

AMERICAN DEMOGRAPHICS BOOKS.

A Division of American Demographics, Inc.
127 West State Street, Ithaca, NY 14850
Telephone: 607-273-6343

Executive Editor: Diane Crispell
Associate Editor: Shannon Dortch
Publisher: Wade Leftwich
Associate Publisher: James Madden
Marketing Associate: Matthew Klein

Copyright © 1995, AMERICAN DEMOGRAPHICS BOOKS
First published USA 1995

All rights reserved. No part of this book may be reproduced, stored in a retrieval system, or transmitted in any form or by any means, electronic, mechanical, photocopying, recording, or otherwise, without the prior written permission of the publisher and the copyright holder. Further information may be obtained from American Demographics, P.O. Box 68, Ithaca, NY 14851.

This publication is designed to provide accurate and authoritative information in regard to the subject matter covered. It is sold with the understanding that the publisher is not engaged in rendering legal, accounting, or other professional services. If legal advice or other expert assistance is required, the services of a competent professional should be sought.

Library of Congress Catalog Number: 94-079-023

Cataloging In Publication Data
Mogelonsky, Marcia 1954–
Everybody Eats

Hardcover: ISBN 0-936889-31-4
Paperback: ISBN 0-936889-32-2

Book design and composition: Paperwork

Contents

Preface

I N THEIR excellent book, *The One to One Future: Building Relationships One Customer at a Time,* Don Peppers and Martha Rogers suggest that a store has two basic functions—to provide a location at which an item can be purchased, and to facilitate the exchange of information by providing a venue in which a buyer can learn more about a product.

But supermarkets provide more than products and product information. They are also social centers, community bulletin boards, restaurants, recycling centers, and even singles' clubs. They are active participants in community affairs and ardent contributors to community welfare. They educate school children and assist mature shoppers. They fulfill a myriad of functions that extend beyond their primary mandate, but only if the people who run supermarkets are in sync with the people who shop at them.

Everyone eats, and almost everyone shops for food. And nearly everyone has an opinion about both supermarkets and shopping. When I told friends and colleagues I was writing a book about the supermarket industry, I was flooded with comments concerning the relative merits of one local store versus another, about which products and services were best and which were worst, and about the universal desire for shorter checkout lines. Both men and women entered into discussions about scanners, food safety, package labels, and food prices.

As Americans become more health-conscious, and as other issues regarding food—supply, cost, availability, and safety—are highlighted by media, food stores are being closely scrutinized. People want to know more about food, and they look to supermarkets to provide them with this information. Consumers also have high expectations of their food stores, and they want to be assured that they can buy the safest, highest quality food at the most reasonable price.

Supermarkets must serve their constituencies. As America changes, neighborhoods change. So do styles, tastes, and fads. For a supermarketer, it is no longer a question of keeping up with the Joneses, but also keeping tabs on the Smiths, the Washingtons, the Sanchezes, the Wus, the Schwartzes, the Chins, and the Molinaris.

This book is meant to help food retailers, advertisers, and manufacturers understand what people want when they make their weekly visit to the grocery store. Different segments of the population look for different products, services, and departments. Knowing which groups make up the clientele of a food store, and learning about those groups' distinguishing characteristics, make it easier for a retailer, an advertiser, or a manufacturer to hit the right mark.

The first part of this book focuses on age-specific groups—mature shoppers, middle-aged shoppers, young adults, teenagers, and children. There are, of course, inevitable overlaps between groups. Middle-aged shoppers are often shopping for children as well, for example, and sometimes for elderly parents. Age groups are not clear-cut either, and the dividing lines between them are not seamless. The youngest members of one group may feel more comfortable with the oldest members of the group behind them; the oldest members of a segment may align themselves more closely with the population ahead of them.

The second part of the book segments supermarket shoppers by ethnicity/race and regionality. This layer of targeting looks at certain traits people of all age cohorts may have in common. Shopping habits may be similar within an ethnic group regardless of age. People in one part of the country may have different requirements or expectations than shoppers in other regions.Taken together, this book presents a survey of the shopping public—our eating habits, our shopping habits, what we are looking for in the food store, how we feel about certain food-related issues, and how the way we live influences the way we approach the ubiquitous task of providing food for ourselves and our families. Given the changing attitudes of supermarket shoppers, it is next to impossible to mention every aspect of the industry. However, this treatment strives to be both comprehensive and concise. To that end, I have received the assistance of a number of companies and individuals, many of whom are mentioned below. I thank them once again for sharing their expertise and proprietary data. Any omissions, misrepresentations, or errors are exclusively my own.

MARCIA MOGELONSKY
Ithaca, New York
October 1994

Acknowledgments

A GREAT number of people have made this book possible. My first debt is to the people at American Demographics—Peter Francese, Jim Madden, Diane Crispell, Brad Edmondson, Wade Leftwich, Shannon Dortch, and everyone else who was there to answer questions, offer guidance, and encourage me every step of the way.

I would especially like to thank Judith Waldrop of American Demographics, whose editorial assistance has been invaluable. I would also like to thank Deborah Bosanko for her help in preparing the graphics that appear in the text, and Caroline Arthur for her careful fact-checking.

While writing this book, I have benefitted from the opinions and expertise of a number of people. Although it is not possible to thank everyone, I would like to mention Ed Russell of the Campbell Soup Company, Camden, New Jersey; Linda Gilbert of HealthFocus, Des Moines; Chris Wolf and John Scroggins of The Food Channel, Chicago; Tom Pirko of Bevmark, Inc., New York City; C. J. Nielsen of Millstone Whole Bean Coffees, Everett, Washington; Sandy Goldman of Shopper-Vision, Norcross, Georgia; and George P. Moschis, professor of marketing at Georgia State University.

I am also grateful to the following people and corporations for giving me access to up-to-the-minute data concerning food products and food shoppers: Irma Zandl of The Zandl Group, New York City; Jay Gangi of Yankelovich Partners, Westport, Connecticut; Gary Berman of Market Segment Research, Inc., Coral Gables, Florida; Catalina Information Resources, Inc., Anaheim, California; Information Resources, Inc., Chicago; Elizabeth Scanlon of Edelman Public Relations, Chicago; and Kathy Mancini of Nielsen Consumer Information Services, Port Washington, New York.

My first experience with the supermarket industry came about as a result of my freelance editing and writing for Cornell University's Home Study Program, a division of the Department of Agricultural Economics. Thanks to "Bud" Hayward, Janelle Tauer, and Nancy Campbell for all their advice and help through the years. I also owe a huge debt to Tim Bumgardner, formerly the managing editor for the Home Study Program, whose friendship has been unflagging.

Cheryl Russell, former editor of *American Demographics* magazine, has provided invaluable help and encouragement. I also want to thank Penelope Wickham of New Strategist Books in Ithaca, and Susan Krafft, formerly of Ithaca, for their encouragement. Nancy Flynn, fellow writer and food shopper, has been a great supporter throughout this project.

The Canadian research team of Ronna Mogelon, Larry and Maureen Mogelonsky, and Alex and Lila Mogelon has worked hard to keep me up-to-date with trends north of the border. A special word of thanks goes to my parents, Alex and Lila, who have been constant cheerleaders. Their freelance careers have inspired my own.

My father-in-law, Aaron Strauss, former market research director of CPC International, and my mother-in-law Diane have been constant sources of advice and encouragement.

Finally, I must thank my husband, Barry Strauss, without whom this book would never have been anything more than an idea. Not to be forgotten are my wonderful children, Sylvie and Michael, who understand that their mother occasionally needs quiet time.

SECTION 1

age, lifestage, and generations

CHAPTER 1

Targeting the Food Shopper
the 1990s and beyond

L IFE WAS easier in the 1950s and 1960s. At least that's what June Cleaver and her friends on Nick at Nite want us to believe. The whole country was middle class—healthy, wealthy, and wise. In the America of reruns, we ate what we wanted. Families always had a full sit-down breakfast—eggs, bacon, cereal, toast with butter, and lots of whole milk. After the kids ran for the school bus, the men went to work and the women went shopping.

When Mom had a bridge luncheon or get-together with the gals, she served cute little party sandwiches and coffee. Dad had a businessman's lunch with a couple of martinis and the kids had peanut butter and jelly on white bread. We all had supper together: meat, potatoes, maybe a green vegetable or a salad, and ice cream. We snacked, too, on chips and peanuts and popcorn with lots of melted butter.

No one ever told us that all that food was bad for us. We were not obsessed with nutrition and health issues. There were no "dangerous" foods. We ate cookies made with coconut and palm oil, pie crust made with lard, and all the red meat we liked. Only women admitted to counting calories, and cholesterol was nothing more than a word in a statewide spelling bee. Food-related health issues never made front-page news.

In the world of the 1950s and 1960s, Mom took the kids to the supermarket after school or on Saturday mornings. The grocery store was a fabulous place. Shelves were stocked with 6,000 products—and not just food. Stores began to offer toys, records, books, school supplies, and housewares.

Not only were there a zillion things to buy, there were also a zillion supermarkets in which to buy them. In 1950, an average of three supermarkets opened every day. Competition was fierce as chains and independents vied for every customer and every customer dollar. Stores opened new departments, added product lines, and offered incentives to keep customers loyal.

Trading stamps, which could be redeemed in exchange for gifts such as patio furniture and barbecue grills, became popular drawing cards. Some stores offered self-service departments; others advertised the service nature of the business. The challenge was to attract a loyal customer base and keep it.

How is this different from the supermarket of today? The need to keep loyal customers happy and to attract new ones is still of paramount importance. Customers still want clean stores and low prices. But customers are not the same people they were in the 1950s and 1960s. Except for the fact that we all still have to eat, just about everything has changed.

❚❚❚ MOVING ON, UP, OUT, AND IN

Supermarkets were built to serve the needs of GIs coming home after World War II. They began in the suburbs. But suburbs are living, breathing organisms. They change with the ebb and flow of the people who inhabit them. And supermarkets must adapt to the changing needs of the neighborhoods they serve.

Some of the neighborhoods that baby boomers grew up in during the 1960s are retirement communities in the 1990s. Others have been infiltrated by new generations, raising children of their own. Some suburbs have changed from white to African American or Asian. Others have gone from WASP to Jewish to Islamic. A few have kept the status quo.

New suburbs are still being built every day. Community associations have formed to ensure that suburbanites have the best of all living conditions. Retirement communities, designed with safety and health features built in, are flourishing as maturing baby boomers realize that there is more of their lives behind them than ahead of them. People are still having kids. And they too are looking for communities that are safe, secure, and comfortable.

Not all the changes have been in the suburbs. Urban areas have also seen great population shifts during the 1980s. New immigrants have moved in. Some inner city areas have been gentrified, while others have been left to decay. Some urban areas have grown, but many have become smaller as residents move to suburbs, exurbs, or small towns. Between 1980 and 1990, two of the 20 largest metropolitan areas (Pittsburgh and Detroit) five got smaller; two increased their population by over 25 percent (San Diego, Phoenix, Dallas-Ft. Worth, Atlanta, and Los Angeles-Anaheim-Riverside).

Both suburbs and their urban cores have become more diverse. The African-American population increased by 40 percent or more between 1980 and 1990 in the Atlanta, Miami-Fort Lauderdale, San Diego, Orlando, Seattle-Tacoma, and Sacramento metropolitan areas. The Hispanic population of Dallas-Fort Worth, Washington, D.C., Boston, Las Vegas, Modesto (California), Atlanta, Springfield (Massachusetts), Providence, and West Palm Beach has more than doubled. In Orlando, Hispanics have nearly tripled. Asian Americans have also increased dramatically. During the 1980s, the Asian population at least doubled in 37 of the 50 metropolitan areas with the most Asians. In four cities—Atlanta, Modesto, Austin, and Merced—the Asian population quadrupled.

I I ■ FOOD AND FAMILY

The changes that have taken place in the American suburbs echo the changes that have taken place in the American family. Even the term "family" has undergone a metamorphosis.

Metropolitan Minorities

Marketers must take into account the characteristics of the neighborhoods they serve. In Baltimore, one in four residents is black; in Miami, one in three is Hispanic; and in San Francisco, one in seven is Asian. But marketers in Minneapolis/St. Paul have few minorities to deal with.

(percent of population by race and Hispanic origin in the 20 largest metropolitan areas, 1990)

metro area	total population
New York-Northern New Jersey-Long Island, NY-NJ-CT-PA, CMSA	8,087 ......
Los Angeles-Anaheim-Riverside, CA, CMSA	8,547 ......
Chicago-Gary-Lake County, IL-IN-WI, CMSA	8,066 ......
San Francisco-Oakland-San Jose, CA CMSA	6,253 ......
Philadelphia-Wilmington-Trenton, PA-NJ-DE-MD CMSA	5,899 ......
Detroit-Ann Arbor, MI CMSA	4,665 ......
Boston-Lawrence-Salem, MA-NH CMSA	4,172 ......
Washington, DC-MD-VA MSA	3,924 ......
Dallas-Fort Worth, TX CMSA	3,885 ......
Houston-Galvwaron-Brazoria, TX CMSA	3,711 ......
Miami-Fort Lauderdale, FL CMSA	3,193 ......
Atlanta, GA MSA	2,834 ......
Cleveland-Akron-Lorain, OH CMSA	2,760 ......
Seattle-Tacoma, WA CMSA	2,559 ......
San DIego, CA MSA	2,498 ......
Minneapolis-St. Paul, MN-WI MSA	2,464 ......
St. Louis, MO-IL MSA	2,444 ......
Baltmore, MD MSA	2,382 ......
Pittsburgh-Beaver Valley, PA CMSA	2,243 ......
Phoenix, AZ MSA	2,122 ......
Tampa St. Petersbutg-Clearwater, FL MSA	2,068 ......
Denver-Boulder, CO CMSA	1,848 ......
Cincinnati-Hamilton, OH-KY-IN CMSA	1,744 ......
Milwaukee-Racine, WI CMSA	1,607 ......
Kansas City, MO-KS MSA	1,566 ......

*Hispanics may be of any race

	white	black	American Indian	Asian	other	Hispanic origin*
....	70.2%	18.2%	0.3%	4.8%	6.5%	15.4%
....	64.6	8.5	0.6	9.2	17.1	32.9
....	71.6	19.2	0.2	3.2	5.9	11.1
....	69.3	8.6	0.7	14.8	6.6	15.5
....	76.9	18.7	0.2	2.1	2.1	3.8
....	76.5	20.9	0.4	1.5	0.7	1.9
....	88.9	5.7	0.2	2.9	2.3	4.6
....	65.7	26.6	0.3	5.2	2.3	5.7
....	75.2	14.3	0.5	2.5	7.5	13.4
....	67.6	17.9	0.3	3.6	10.6	20.8
....	76.4	18.5	0.2	1.4	3.6	33.3
....	71.3	26.0	0.2	1.8	0.7	2.0
....	82.0	16.0	0.2	1.0	0.8	1.9
....	86.4	4.8	1.3	6.4	1.1	3.0
....	75.0	6.4	0.8	7.9	9.9	20.4
....	92.1	3.6	1.0	2.6	0.6	1.5
....	81.2	17.3	0.2	1.0	0.3	1.1
....	71.7	25.9	0.3	1.8	0.3	1.3
....	91.0	8.0	0.1	0.7	0.2	0.6
....	84.8	3.5	1.8	1.7	8.2	16.3
....	88.4	9.0	0.3	1.1	1.3	6.7
....	86.5	5.3	0.8	2.3	5.1	12.2
....	87.2	11.7	0.1	0.8	0.2	0.5
....	83.1	13.3	0.5	1.2	1.8	3.8
....	84.3	12.8	0.5	1.1	1.3	2.9

Source: Bureau of the Census

If you want to be brought up-to-date on the changes in the American family over the past decade, just check out the greeting-card aisle of your local supermarket. On Mother's Day, alongside cards for dear old mom, there are cards for stepmothers, godmothers, mothers-to-be, father's new wife, and for that special someone "who's been like a mom to me." There are even Mother's Day cards for Dad. Who sends these cards? Stepdaughters, godsons, grandchildren, and grateful mothers who must depend on others for child care.

While the number of family households has increased by almost one-third during the last two decades, the number of married-couple households increased at only half that rate. Family households headed by dads more than tripled and single-mother households more than doubled. Married couples with no children under age 18 increased 45

The Family of the 1990s

Today, nearly one in every four households is a person living alone.
(thousands of households by type, 1970, 1990, and percent change, 1970-90)

type	1990	1970	percent change 1970-90
Total households	93,347	63,401	47.2%
Families	66,090	51,456	28.4
Married couples	52,317	44,728	16.9
with children < 18	24,537	25,532	-3.9
with no children < 18	27,780	19,196	44.7
Single fathers	1,153	341	238.1
Single mothers	6,599	2,858	130.9
Other families	5,991	4,211	42.3
Nonfamilies	27,257	11,945	128.2
Men living alone	9,049	3,532	156.2
Women living alone	13,950	7,319	90.6
Other nonfamilies*	4,258	1,094	289.2

other nonrelated households such as roommates and unmarried partners

Source: Bureau of the Census

percent. But those with young children at home decreased by almost 4 percent. And there are more non-family households* than ever before. More men and women are living alone, and more are sharing accommodations in non-traditional arrangements.

Understanding the way in which household dynamics have changed helps retailers understand their clientele and the products and services they need. Single servings suit single shoppers. Stores in areas in which all the children have grown up and moved out can cut back on sugared cereal. Baby food will move slowly in aging neighborhoods, while in-store pharmacies may flourish. Stores that serve active young people may want to keep their doors open 24 hours a day, while those who serve a working clientele may want to increase the number of cashiers on Saturdays and Sundays. Knowing the demographics of the buying population is the only way to keep up with the changing needs of a store's customers.

I I I NUTRITIONAL CONFUSION

It started with eggs. Suddenly, they just weren't good for you anymore. Then came butter. Butter was bad; margarine was good. But now margarine is bad, too. Popcorn was good; now it's bad, if it's made with coconut oil. Meat was good, then it was bad. Some oils are bad; others are good, if not great. Sugar is good or bad, and artificial sweeteners are good, sometimes. Cauliflower, which was always good, has been elevated to sainthood, and pasta, which was once exotic, is now good, under most circumstances.

Food is a hot topic. Even presidents of the United States speak out for or against certain fruits and vegetables. Broccoli, disdained by President Bush, was empowered by President Clinton, who gave it his full support. One would think that an endorsement from the chief executive would be important to a much-maligned but nutritionally valuable vegetable like broccoli. But considering how much we know about the President's diet and eating habits, skeptics aren't convinced.

The way Americans eat has been changing dramatically over recent decades. The four food groups have been replaced by the food

Nonfamilies include people living alone and other households in which no one is related to the head of household by blood, marriage, or adoption.

pyramid. There are now five major food groups which Americans are urged to eat regularly: meat, milk, vegetables, fruit, and bread. Other foods, fats, oils, and sweets, have been relegated to the topmost part of the pyramid, to save for special occasions.

The food pyramid has its variations. Some nutritionists stress the "Mediterranean" food pyramid, developed in 1994 by the Harvard School of Public Health, Oldways Preservation & Exchange Trust, and the World Health Organization European Regional Office. Based on traditional eating habits in the eastern Mediterranean, southern Italy, and Greece, this system places more value on olive oil than on red meat, and permits adults to consume wine in moderation.

The standard and Mediterranean food pyramids are but two of many different schools of nutrition. Diet books pop up faster than toaster pastries. And for every "eat this," there is a "don't eat that." The Food and Drug Administration, entering the diet and nutrition fray, launched a new system for nutrition labeling of almost all food products in 1994. The new label, which indicates not only the number of calories per serving, but also the percentage of calories from fat, accompanies other labeling regulations that control the use of such words as "low-fat," "lite," "light," and "organic."

All this attention to what we eat has had mixed results. Almost half of Americans are very concerned about the nutritional value of the foods they eat, according to a 1993 *Parade* magazine study. Men voice more concern than women. And older people are especially concerned about food additives and other things in foods they eat. But some people who have been through the diet mill are beginning to lose faith in the food gurus. Many are shying away from health claims, at least until they have been substantiated by years of testing and research. Others who denied themselves the pleasure of full-fat ice cream and high-calorie cookies for years are giving into their urges. Part of the reason is emotional and part is economic. During the recession of the first years of the 1990s, some people denied themselves the pleasures of these consumer products. But food is cheaper than a second car and more practical than a winter cruise; and it's completely satisfying.

"The most important influence on new product development in 1993 was consumers' declining interest in nutritionally enhanced foods, and their parallel return to high fat, high sugar, high calorie, high cholesterol, indulgent eating," according to Lynn Dornblaser, publisher of the Chicago-based *New Product News.*

But Americans—especially aging boomers—are in search of the fountain of youth. Even if that fountain is filled with fat-free, sugar-free, calcium-enhanced, low-calorie, cruciferous vegetable-extracted antioxidants, that may or may not do the trick, it's worth a try.

I I I CHANGING FORTUNES

When boomers were in kindergarten, most of them had one working father and a stay-at-home mother who was available for after-school snack time, team practices, Boy Scouts, ballet, and music lessons. Dad worked from 9 to 5; Mom worked all the time, but only at home. Weekends were spent with the entire family, doing "family things," like going to sports events, visiting relatives, going for a drive, gardening, and grocery shopping. But times have changed. In 1993, 57 percent of women worked outside the home. Even women with young children are likely to have jobs outside the home, whether they are single parents or married.

Women in the workforce have changed the way in which families function on a day-to-day basis. Many children of the 1980s and 1990s are used to coming home to an empty house and fending for themselves. Parents have begun to give more responsibility to their children at a younger age. Teens regularly go to the grocery store for their parents, and even pre-teens are able to prepare their own snacks or meals.

Catering to the needs of the working family requires a host of new products that would seem strange to the mom of the 1950s. The microwave oven, premade and frozen foods, even precut and prewashed vegetables, fruits, and salads have made cooking easier for busy parents who often have little time between coming home from work and sitting down to supper.

Getting a meal prepared, one that will please the whole family, is a challenge. Getting it prepared *quickly* is an even greater feat. More than half (55 percent) of women spend from one-half to one hour preparing dinner, according to a 1993 survey by *Parade* magazine. But if they could, these women would like to be in the kitchen for less than a half hour. With short cuts, like using precooked vegetables, premade pie crusts, and ready-to-serve meats, the time can be reduced.

Eighty-four percent of people who use convenience foods agree they are more expensive than foods that take longer to prepare. Even with the economic downturns, three-quarters of convenience-food users feel the time saved is worth the additional cost. One of the first

Women's Work

Divorced mothers with school-aged children have the highest work rates of all women.

(labor force participation rates of women with children aged 6 to 17, under the age of 6, and with no children, by marital status, 1980, 1990, and 1993, and percent change 1980-93)

status	1993	1990	1980	percent change 1980-93
All women	57.2%	57.2%	51.5%	11.1%
married, spouse present	59.4	58.2	50.1	18.6
divorced	72.7	75.5	74.5	-2.4
separated	60.7	63.6	59.4	2.2
single	64.5	66.4	61.5	4.9
Women with children 6 to 17	75.4	74.7	64.3	17.3
married, spouse present	74.9	73.6	61.7	21.4
divorced	83.6	85.9	82.3	1.6
separated	71.6	75.0	66.3	8.0
single	70.2	69.7	67.6	3.8
Women with children under 6	57.9	58.2	46.8	23.7
married, spouse present	59.6	58.9	45.1	32.2
divorced	68.1	69.8	68.3	-0.3
separated	52.1	59.3	52.2	-0.2
single	47.4	48.7	44.1	7.5
Women with no children under age 18	52.1	52.3	48.1	8.3
married, spouse present	52.4	51.1	46.0	13.9
divorced	69.2	72.2	71.4	-3.1
separated	58.4	59.2	58.9	-0.8
single	66.4	68.1	62.1	6.9

Source: Bureau of Labor Statistics

lessons of Family Economics 101 is understanding the value of time.

Time is important, but so is money. The recession of 1990-91 has taken its toll on the American family. Many baby busters, people born between 1965 and 1976, feel that they are in worse financial shape than their parents were when they were young. Boomers—those of us born between 1946 and 1964—saw their incomes rise in the 1980s, and fall quickly in the early 1990s. Mature consumers who have entered their retirement years are in general well positioned financially, but they have the worries that accompany old age: ensuring that their pension and social security benefits will provide enough income and hoping that debilitating illnesses will not force them to need extended nursing care.

The last recession affected different ethnic groups in different ways. Hispanic men saw their personal income fall by 12 percent in the decade between 1980 and 1990. African-American men saw their personal income increase by slightly more than 1 percent. White men experienced only a 0.1 percent gain. But women saw their personal incomes rise, as more women entered the workforce and the gap between men's and women's earnings narrowed. White women saw their incomes rise by 31 percent. African-American women had only a 15 percent increase. And the increase in personal income for Hispanic women was just about 8 percent during the decade.

Some families that were one-salary households in the 1980s have become two-salary households by necessity in the 1990s; other have become that way by choice. Some families have working teenagers; some are supported solely by a single parent. Almost all saw their incomes fall during the recession of the 1990s, and not everyone has seen his or her income begin to rise in its aftermath. Still, some trend trackers predict that the 1990s will be the most affluent decade in American history.

How has the changing economy affected the way in which people shop for food? More people are more careful about how and where they shop. In 1993, when *Parade* magazine asked shoppers if they were comparison shopping more than in the past, 85 percent said, "yes." In 1991, that figure was 75 percent; in 1989, 67 percent said they were comparison shopping more often. Shoppers are also more likely to use more coupons—68 percent in 1993, compared with 66 percent in 1991, and 56 percent in 1989.

After adjusting for inflation, average weekly family grocery spending increased from $64 in 1984 to a high of $80 in 1993, but dropped to $79 in 1994, according to a study by the Washington, D.C.-based

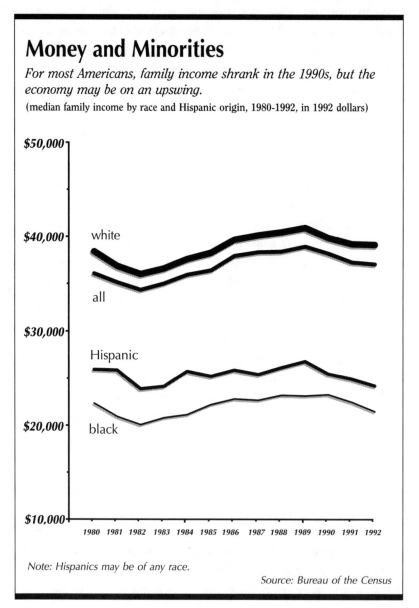

Money and Minorities

For most Americans, family income shrank in the 1990s, but the economy may be on an upswing.

(median family income by race and Hispanic origin, 1980-1992, in 1992 dollars)

Note: Hispanics may be of any race.

Source: Bureau of the Census

Food Marketing Institute (FMI). The survey found that consumers are using a number of techniques to help keep their grocery expenses down, including cents-off coupons and comparison shopping.

That leads to the next lesson in Family Economics 101: how to keep customers happy. The best way is to provide them with good service at a fair price. But while that may seem like just plain common sense, there are a few more factors to take into account. "Price does show up as a big factor in all the studies," according to Len Berry, professor of marketing at Texas A&M University in College Station. "But price means different things to different people. There is a segment that is price-conscious and very price-oriented. This segment is composed of two groups—the ones who are loyal to the store they perceive to be the least expensive, and those shoppers who are 'cherry-pickers'—those who shop around for bargains.

"But," continues Dr. Berry, "In some markets, price competitiveness among retailers can actually cause them to cancel each other out—if all stores in one area are perceived to be similar in price, then consumers will choose other variables on which to make their selection. And that is often the case. In fact, some of the most successful chains in the country are those that may not come out first in a price survey. But they distinguish themselves in other ways—cleanliness, selection, services, and so on."

I I ∎ LOYAL CUSTOMERS

Price-conscious consumers often visit more than one grocery store in search of special prices, a bargain-hunting practice known in the industry as "cherry picking." In order to keep these shoppers from making the rounds, retailers are putting in place a variety of systems to dissuade visits to rival stores. Many of the new strategies take greater advantage of database marketing methods made possible by the advent of electronic price scanning.

In 1994, shoppers averaged 2.1 trips a week to a grocery store, and almost half of these shoppers visited two different stores each week, according to data published by *Progressive Grocer* magazine (Stamford, Connecticut) and the Washington, D.C.-based Food Marketing Institute (FMI).

Over 80 percent of a supermarket's customers shop there less than once a week, according to a recent study conducted for the Coca-Cola Retailing Research Council. Most customers visit a specific store only about once every two weeks. People shop around for convenience and variety. But they are most likely to switch stores when they are looking for good deals. With so many customers looking for bargains at so many different stores, it is no wonder that the average supermarket company loses between 25 and 50 percent of its customers each year. In order to lure customers, supermarketers have until recently relied primarily on one of two pricing strategies: weekly specials or EDLP (everyday low prices). But new technologies have encouraged marketers to try a host of other tactics.

With the advent of scanning technology, a third pricing strategy is being tried. Called Customer Specific Pricing (CSP), this system rewards frequent and loyal customers. Instead of offering the same specials and discounts to every shopper, CSP identifies and compensates customers depending on their past shopping patterns and their potential value to the retailer.

A supermarket's best customers shop there more often each week, and spend more on each visit, than the average patron, according to a study by Coca-Cola. In one store, for example, the top ten percent of customers visited the store an average of 1.78 times per week and accounted for 43 percent of the store's weekly sales. Rewarding these kinds of customers is increasingly viewed as more important than attracting new—and potentially fickle—shoppers by offering them the same deals as the loyal and lucrative few.

What makes this type of program work is the "Frequent Shopper Card" that retailers give free of charge to any customer who applies. These bar-coded cards, which are scanned along with the items purchased, track the purchasing habits of customers. They also record the shopper's identity so that he or she can be targeted for unadvertised specials.

A CSP program was recently implemented in the Snyder Foods Stores in Oklahoma City. The company stopped offering "double coupons"—a system by which all manufacturers' coupons were redeemed at double their face value—and weekly specials to all of its customers.

Instead, the stores distributed their own coupons—with a difference. Loyal customers received coupons worth more than those given to infrequent shoppers. The program garnered increased customer support, and encouraged shoppers to stay loyal to Snyder.

Identifying and targeting the frequent shopper helps supermarketers to build and maintain a loyal following. A common customer complaint is that supermarkets do nothing more for loyal shoppers than they do for infrequent shoppers, according to Brian P. Woolf, president of the Greenville, South Carolina-based Retail Strategy Center, Inc., the principal investigator for the Coca-Cola Retailing Research Council's study. By making them members of an exclusive club, one that has definite monetary rewards, supermarketers are rewarding their special customers. And the customers in turn will reward the retailer with even more frequent visits.

Still Number One

Cereals and breakfast foods were the first type of product to be promoted through couponing, and they're still number one.

(top-ranked product categories for coupon distribution, 1991-92)

product category	1992	1991
Cereals and breakfast food	1	1
Candy and gum	2	4
Medications, remedies, health aids	3	2
Pet food	4	5
Sanitary protection	5	6
Detergents	6	8
Hair care products	7	11
Cookies, crackers	8	7
Household cleaners	9	12
Cough/cold remedies	10	3

Source: NCH Promotional Services: Food Institute
"Food Retailing Reviews" 1994

▌▌▌ COUPON CLIPPERS

Coupons are big business. And with the advent of scanning technology, they are getting even bigger. The first documented coupon in this country came from C.W. Post, the Battle Creek-based cereal manufacturer. In 1895, the company launched its new health cereal, Grape Nuts, and gave customers a coupon to save one cent on their next product purchase.

It wasn't until the golden era of the 1950s that couponing became an organized marketing strategy. Marketers realized that they had to entice customers to try new products. And what better way to get someone to try something than to offer it for nothing—or close to nothing. The earliest players in the coupon game were Procter & Gamble, General Foods, Lever Brothers, General Mills, Scott Paper Company, and A.C. Nielsen.

Coupons increased in popularity throughout the 1950s and 1960s. When NCH Promotional Services began to track coupons in 1965, some 10 million were distributed annually. In 1993, 298.5 billion coupons were distributed—down 3.7 percent from 1992. It was the first decline since 1970.

Why do consumers use coupons? Some need an incentive to try a new product. About 13,000 food products are launched annually—and they sink or swim only with the backing of consumers. If a customer is given a coupon, he or she is more likely to try out a new product. "Why should I pay for it? I may not like it, and that would be a waste of money," is a commonly expressed sentiment. But if the product can be purchased for 50 cents, 75 cents, or even a dollar less, a customer is more willing to take a chance.

The main reason that customers use coupons is to save money on products they use regularly. In 1993, the average face value of a redeemed coupon rose to 59.5 cents, a record high. That year, consumers saved a total of $4 billion using coupons, a figure topped only by 1992's record $4.5 billion.

Coupon distribution and use have declined in part because manufacturers are experimenting. Some, like Procter & Gamble, have put EDLP (everyday low prices) ahead of coupon discounts in their marketing strategy. P & G virtually stopped offering cents-off coupons on disposable diapers, finding that selling the product at a lower price consistently was helping to alleviate some of the losses in the category due to the increasing popularity of store-brand and private-label diapers.

In general, there has been a reduction in the number of high-value coupons distributed in big categories such as diapers and detergent. But the other factor that leaves more coupons on the counter than in the store is their increasingly short expiration dates. The average redemption period in 1993 was 3.8 months, compared with 4 months in 1992 and a high of 7.6 months in 1988, according to Carolina Manufacturers Service of Winston-Salem, North Carolina.

I ∎ HIGH-TECH COUPONING

The coupon industry has become as high tech as almost every other facet of the supermarket. Consumers can still clip coupons from advertising inserts in the Sunday paper. They can also check out circulars from their local supermarkets to take advantage of store savings. But new technologies are making it possible to collect even more coupons for even greater savings.

Electronic technology makes it easier to ensure that coupons get into the hands of people most likely to use them. The St. Petersburg-based Catalina Marketing Corporation, for example, supplies in-store electronic scanner-activated coupons in a product known as Checkout Coupon. These purchase-activated coupons are generated based on the products that a shopper buys.

Checkout Coupon can be used by retailers and manufacturers in a number of ways. Incentives can be issued to users of competitive brands within a product category—for example, a shopper buying Brand X peanut butter may be issued a coupon for Brand Y peanut butter at the checkout. Coupons for complementary products or brands may be offered—the peanut butter buyer may get a coupon for grape jelly at the checkout. Or he may get a coupon to reward him for buying Brand X peanut butter—one worth cents off his next purchase of the same product. He may also get a coupon to entice him to buy a larger jar of Brand X or a different flavor of Brand X peanut butter—crunchy instead of smooth, for example.

Electronic checkout coupons don't even have to be on paper.

Some supermarkets have begun to advertise "clipless coupons" for holders of their Frequent Shopper cards. These stores still advertise their weekly specials in newspapers and circulars, but they do not offer all of the specials to all of their shoppers. Instead, some specials, advertised in a coupon-style graphic in the circular, are available only to customers with Frequent Shopper cards. The cents-off value of the special is automatically deducted from a card-holding shopper's total when all of her purchases have been scanned. The shopper does not have to clip and present the coupon in order to get the discount, and only shoppers with cards can enjoy the savings.

But coupon users should not retire the scissors yet, according to Jane Perrin of NCH Promotional Services, Dun & Bradstreet's promotional information division. "It's not like the coupon is going to go away. There are nearly 7 billion pieces of paper out there that consumers have been clipping. They're still reliant on paper coupons. It helps consumers shop and plan, whereas the paperless coupon is more in-store motivated," she asserts.

Targeting coupon users is becoming increasingly sophisticated. Companies that maintain extensive databases on households to which their coupons are distributed can make sure that a dog owner receives free samples of puppy treats, while at the same time, her cat-loving next-door neighbor gets free samples of kitty food. Donnelley Marketing Inc.'s Carol Wright division, which distributes coupons through the mail, maintains a database on 87 million households. The company sends ten mailings a year to 30 million households, custom-designing the offerings to match the consumers' lifestyles.

Another value-added ploy for retailers is to offer "double coupons," a program that is popular in areas in which competition between chains is fierce. Supermarkets that offer double coupons will redeem coupons at twice their face value. The first half of the savings comes from the manufacturer who issued the coupon. The second half comes from the supermarket, which must cut into its profits to give the customer his or her additional savings.

Almost three-quarters of grocery shoppers almost always look over their coupons before they go shopping, according to *Progressive Grocer* magazine's 1994 annual report. Forty-seven percent are using coupons more than they did a year ago. The most popular coupons are those for breakfast cereal, bathroom supplies, kitchen items, over-the-counter medications, and beauty aids. And the higher the better, consumers maintain. Some shoppers won't even waste time clipping a coupon that has a value of 20 cents or less. But if the 20-cent saving is deducted automatically through a clipless coupon, no one is going to complain. They won't complain, but will they even notice? Why do manufacturers and retailers bother with coupons of such low value? "It is the effort involved in the savings that makes a difference to most people," says P. Rajan Varadarajan, Foleys Professor of Retailing and Marketing at Texas A&M University in College Station. "If there is no incremental effort but there are some savings, shoppers will be happy. If, on the other hand, a shopper has to clip a coupon—and remember to take it to the store—all in order to save 20 cents, he or she will not bother."

I I ■ MORE THAN LOW PRICES

Another way in which retailers can improve customer loyalty is by finding a cause that customers believe in and setting up a program to benefit that cause. Many shoppers like to know that the store in which they buy their groceries is an active and enthusiastic supporter of the community. Supporting a cause such as recycling, protecting the environment, helping local schools, and even supporting local sports teams is a good way to show community involvement.

The Springfield, Massachusetts-based Big Y chose education as its focus for a customer participation program. In 1992, the company implemented a program called "Education Express." Frequent Shopper cardholders were invited to sign up for the program and designate a school they wished to support. Each week, a number of products in the store were designated as "Education Express" items. Every time a participating customer purchased one of these items, her designated school earned points which could be used for the purchase of various types of equipment, ranging from computers to musical instruments.

Programs to benefit education have been implemented in supermarkets in other cities. In many cases, however, the programs are labor intensive, for both participating shoppers and schools. Register tapes have to be collected and tallied by hand—requiring work by teachers or PTA members—and participating shoppers often forget to save the register tapes or to give them to the schools in the allotted time. By using electronic data collection methods, Big Y's program was easy to use and successful, earning close to $2 million in equipment for local schools.

Other causes that supermarkets can target include building playground equipment, helping day care centers, paying for park clean-ups, or supporting senior citizen programs. By choosing a cause that focuses on the community and community-based issues and interests, the retailer is guaranteed the support of a loyal customer base—at least until the program is over. Keeping the customers returning after that requires other marketing strategies.

Retailers have used a variety of incentives to encourage customers to become frequent shoppers. Some stores have collaborated with other operators to make it possible for Frequent Customer cardholders to get discounts at local amusement parks, zoos, or other attractions.

Other retailers have special newsletters for cardholders or kids' clubs for cardholders' children. The 23-store, Richmond, Virginia-based Ukrops Company has built a database of some 225,000 households, from which it can target specific customers based on the information they provide in their Frequent Customer card applications.

Big Y Markets has found another way of encouraging frequent shoppers. In 1994, the company launched its "Express Millions" incentive, in which card-holding customers are entered in a sweepstakes contest every time their cards are scanned. The grand prize is $1 million, and there is no limit to the number of times a customer can enter.

Imaginative programs like this are essential given the highly competitive nature of the retail grocery business. Double and triple couponing, deep discounts on seasonal items, contests, and incentives have been commonplace in the industry for years. It is the electronic revolution that has made it easier for retailers to implement a host of attractive savings programs, and for customers to reap their benefits.

I ∎ THE SUPERMARKET OF THE FUTURE

In her 1970 forecast for the supermarket industry, Jennifer Cross, author of *The Supermarket Trap: The Consumer and the Food Industry,* predicted the state of the supermarket by the year 2000. Asserting that "in about fifteen years, the present 'wheel of retailing' is due to end," she predicted that afterwards, "anything can happen."

Cross described some of the potential supermarket formats that could be in place by the end of the century. "One... is the automat, a superior version of Horn & Hardart, where the customer either drives her car or walks onto a moving ramp, is conveyed decorously through the whole store, selects her groceries by viewing samples displayed in lighted wall panels (or unlocking the cases with a special key on her credit card), and chooses her meat and produce via closed-circuit TV. She then drives around to a separate warehouse area to collect her order, paid for by a universal credit-card system. Such an emporium would probably be multi-storey to help solve the space problem. Most of the people would be invisible, except for the customers."

Cross' vision of the supermarket circa 1985 to 2000 sounds like a 1960s "Star Trek" episode, even in 1994. But even in this fanciful reconstruction, she has hit upon some of the features consumers want in a supermarket. Convenience, the ability to get groceries whenever one wants, is important to shoppers, and supermarkets are staying open longer to accommodate them. The average supermarket was open 130 hours per week in 1993, according to *Progressive Grocer* magazine. Almost all stores are open seven days a week, and 34 percent offer round-the-clock shopping.

Cross' vision of shoppers paying with a universal credit card is a reality in about half of supermarkets, and 31 percent accept debit cards. But that's about as far as comparisons between Cross' store of the future and the store of the present can go. There are no moving sidewalks— although many women who shop at the end of a busy work day would welcome them. There are still plenty of people in the supermarket— and not just customers. Service departments—in-store delis, bakeries, cheese counters—are offered by a majority of stores, and customers in the store of the 1990s can order meat, produce, bread, and deli items from real people, not from automats.

Consumers also want cleanliness, witnessed by Cross' product-free future supermarket. In her scenario, the customer never gets to see the real food product he or she wants to buy. Without having to actually stock shelves with groceries or set up fresh displays of perishables that can be handled by customers, the store will certainly stay clean. But customers want to be able to see what they are buying, to squeeze the tomatoes, sniff the fish, and examine the steak. Because shopping is a hands-on experience, and will remain one as long as our obsession with food continues, the product-free store of Cross' future will be a long time coming.

Perhaps the biggest contrast is Cross' vision of the supermarket as an automated, people-free zone. In reality, many supermarkets have become gathering places, not empty spaces. Mature shoppers can meet friends, sit at an in-store coffee bar or restaurant, and chat while waiting for a prescription to be filled. Young people who are perhaps shopping for themselves for the first time congregate in the food court or in-store restaurant after a busy day. And working women and men can bring their children to the supermarket on a weekend to shop among the crowds of other working parents and children.

More supermarkets are offering services that will keep shoppers in the store—food courts, sit down eating, salad bars, fruit/juice bars, and hot food bars. Taking a cue from fast-food restaurants, many stores have combined their food-at-home profile with a food-away-from-home feature, so that busy shoppers can buy groceries to use during the week and eat a meal in the same place. The store has become more of a social center than ever before.

❚❚❚ FUTURE SHOCK NOW

Another of Cross' predictions for the future involves the teleshop, where each family "orders from home via closed-circuit TV, and their groceries are delivered in person, or via some (admittedly science fiction) system of pneumatic tubes." This futurist vision may have seemed more far-fetched to Cross than her automat store, but she was on the right track. In 1994, Time Warner Cable and ShopperVision, Inc. of Norcross, Georgia, introduced "virtual grocery shopping" to cable subscribers in Orlando.

With this service, customers can stay at home and shop the total supermarket (with the Supermarket Channel) or drugstore (with the Drugstore Channel). They can "walk" down aisles projected on their television screen, choose products they want, and even "pick up" certain items and turn them around to read nutrition labels and other information—all by using remote controls.

The groceries are sold at local market prices, and shoppers can choose the participating supermarket at which they want to shop. They can even access coupons through the interactive program, or call up their last grocery order to see what they bought previously. A running tally of purchases is kept so that shoppers can know exactly what they have spent.

When the groceries have been purchased and paid for, they are delivered—not by pneumatic tubes—but by truck or van, or shoppers arrange to have them picked up. Shoppers can pay for their groceries with credit cards—right on the screen—or with cash or check when the items are delivered or picked up. The service is free, except for a delivery charge, and Time Warner hopes to extend the service to cable subscribers in some 36 states.

"The system should appeal to a number of demographic groups," according to Sandy Goldman, president of ShopperVision, Inc. "Busy, dual-income couples will want to take advantage of it. People with young kids who don't want to take the children to the supermarket will be able to shop from home. And the mature or disabled shopper will have the independence of being able to shop alone."

But what about the melon squeezers? "People who hate to shop will probably use the service for all their grocery needs," says Goldman. "The quality and freshness of perishables such as meat and produce are guaranteed. If a shopper is not happy, he or she can return an item. But people who really don't mind shopping too much may use the service to buy the more mundane products and leave their shopping time free for purchasing produce, meat, and other fresh goods."

▮▮ THE SUPERMARKET OF THE PRESENT

Grocery shopping may not be anyone's idea of a fun activity. In fact, most people complain about it. But everyone eats, and most everyone shops.

A 1991 *Progressive Grocer* survey asked shoppers to rate the trustworthiness of a variety of public and private institutions on a scale of 1 to 10, with a rating of 1 signifying "not trustworthy" and 10 indicating "extremely trustworthy." Of the nine choices, the highest ranked was "your supermarket," with a rating of 7.54. "Your supermarket" outranked banks (rating of 7.2), supermarkets in general (6.65), hospitals (5.85), government (4.42), and the media (4.28).

Since that survey, consumers have remained more or less happy with their supermarkets—shoppers gave their primary store a rating of 7.5 on a scale of 10 (with 10 being "sensational" and 1 being "awful") in *Progressive Grocer*'s 1994 annual report. Consumers are looking for cleanliness, low prices, pleasant, accurate checkout clerks, food, produce and meat departments, and convenient store location when they choose a food store, just as they did in the 1950s. But in the technologically-driven 1990s, they are also looking for accurate price scanning.

And supermarketers have been working hard in times of economic and social insecurity to provide the services their constituencies want. More stores offer more services than ever before—from fax ordering to catering, from sit-down eating to home delivery, stores are working hard to please all of the shoppers all of the time. The trick for marketers is to understand the changes that may have taken place in their community, and to know who the shoppers are and what they want, even as they change.

CHAPTER 2

The Mature Market
growing stronger every day

B ECAUSE of their growing numbers and special needs, mature Americans will constitute a powerful economic, social, and political force in the coming decades. In 1990, 52.3 million Americans were aged 55 and older. Between 1990 and 2000, the number will increase 12 percent, while the population in general will increase only 11 percent, according to the Bureau of the Census. Older Americans account for 21 percent of the U.S. population now, but by 2020, they will represent 29 percent of all Americans.

For the most part, older Americans will be retired. But that doesn't mean they're living on fixed incomes. Between 1980 and 1993, the median income of households headed by someone aged 65 and older rose from $15,000 (in 1992 dollars) to $17,160. Poverty levels for the elderly have decreased, and their economic status has increased.

Medical advances can assure mature Americans a longer, and in most cases, healthier future. In 1900, a 65-year-old person could expect to live only 12 more years—to age 77. By 1990, life expectancy at age

65 increased another 5 years—to age 82. Many older adults no longer have dependents living with them—although some share their time and wealth with their children and grandchildren. Both older single women and older married couples rank grandchildren as their most important lifestyle activity, according to Standard Rates and Data Services' *Lifestyle Market Analyst*. Targeting the mature market requires more than stocking up on Geritol and arthritis pain medication.

It is difficult to categorize or subdivide the mature market. And it seems that almost every researcher has a different definition. For the purposes of this book, the mature market includes people aged 55 and older; seniors are defined as people aged 65 and older.

Group Portrait

The number of persons aged 85 and older will almost double from 1980 to 2000.

(the mature population, in thousands, by age, 1980, 1990, and 2000)

age	1980	1990	2000
55 to 64	21,703	21,112	23,988
65 to 74	15,582	18,045	18,258
75 to 84	7,729	10,012	12,339
85+	2,240	3,021	4,289

Source: Bureau of the Census

ⅠⅠ MATURE SPENDING

In general, mature Americans spend less than younger householders for food. Household size plays a large role in this decline with age. Most younger families are buying food for one or more children, but older households are often child-free. In 1992, the average number of people in a household or consumer unit* in the 35- to 44-year-old age group is 3.2. It is 2.4 for those aged 55 to 64, 1.8 for those aged 65 to 74, and

*The Bureau of Labor Statistics' consumer units are not exactly comparable to households as defined by the Bureau of the Census.

just 1.6 for those aged 75 and older, according to the Bureau of Labor Statistics' Consumer Expenditure Survey (CE).

It is not only diet and health that may influence shopping choices, but living situation as well. While households aged 35 to 44 spend about $28 a year per capita on frozen meals, households aged 65 to 74 spend an average of almost $26, according to the CE. Convenience and product size are the main reasons older Americans rely on prepared frozen foods. With fewer people to cook for, preparing a frozen meal is a time- and money-saving solution.

Other categories in which households aged 65 and older spend more per capita than others are roast beef, artificial sweeteners, and coffee. The difference is marginal for most of these items, but older shoppers spend twice as much as younger shoppers on coffee each year. The coffee habit, fed by years of on-the-job java, is a tough one to break.

Households aged 55 to 64 spend less per capita than households in general on products such as rice, some beef products, pork chops,

The Mature Market Basket

Mature households spend less than average on many food items, but spend more on bread, fresh fruit, vegetables, and coffee.

(average annual household expenditures for selected grocery products, by age, 1992)

product	all households	55 to 64	65 to 74	75+
Fresh fruit	$127.39	$154.41	$134.68	$123.64
Milk & cream	133.81	127.91	111.93	118.35
Fresh vegetables	126.58	142.69	131.61	101.62
Poultry	123.10	132.48	119.87	81.90
Ground beef	86.66	80.16	72.52	51.99
Bread	76.28	79.53	79.58	66.41
Potato chips/nuts/snacks	75.64	73.70	55.11	40.31
Nonprescription drugs	74.51	77.77	97.77	103.25
Toilet paper/tissues	56.62	59.83	66.87	47.08
Coffee	38.95	53.19	48.01	38.02

Source: Bureau of Labor Statistics, 1992 Consumer Expenditure Survey

lamb, fresh milk and cream, frozen fruit and fruit juices, and non-carbonated fruit-flavored drinks. Households aged 55 to 64 spend less per capita than households in general on sirloin steak, frozen prepared food, potato chips and other snacks, baby food, and cola.

Spending on nonprescription drugs is only about 8 percent higher among households aged 65 and older than for households in general. The big difference lies in prescription drugs, a category in which the older group spends over three times more than the younger one per household. For older adults who look for convenience when shopping, being able to buy medications at their grocery store is a definite plus. Don't assume retired people don't need convenience. After all, many older adults are disabled or lack transportation.

Supermarkets that provide pharmacy services are profiting. In 1992, the prescription-drug category saw an almost 19 percent increase in volume, according to the *Supermarket Business* 46th Annual Consumer Expenditure Study. One-fourth of chains now offer in-store pharmacies, according to *Progressive Grocer*'s 61st Annual Report of the Grocery Industry. But independents may find that providing a pharmacist on the premises is too costly—only 8 percent of independents offer this service.

❙❙❙ MATURE SEGMENTS

While it is tempting to assume that all older adults live on fixed incomes, this view is unrealistic and deceptive. A number of factors influence the amount of discretionary income older Americans have to spend on food and other day-to-day necessities. And the income potential and buying power of the mature market are substantial.

Education, living arrangements, age, and gender all affect the financial situation of older adults. Americans aged 55 and older derive their incomes from more than a dozen sources—including wages and salaries, dividends, self-employment, Social Security, pensions, and trusts, according to Judith Waldrop, research editor of American Demographics.

In 1992, adults aged 55 to 64 had a median household income almost 11 percent higher than households in general. Wages and salaries are the most important source of income for this group. Fully

78 percent of households contain at least one person in the labor force and of those, over 40 percent contain two or more earners. Only 30 percent collect Social Security, and 24 percent get a pension. On the other hand, adults aged 65 to 74 had a median household income almost 32 percent below average. Although most householders in this age group are still married, only 19 percent are headed by active labor-force participants. Instead, the single most important income generator for this segment is Social Security, received by 91 percent of the group. About 45 percent of people in this age cohort also receive money from pensions.

In 1992, householders aged 75 and older had a median household income of $13,993—less than half of the median income for all households. The majority of these households derive their income from Social Security, the mean amount of which was $6,465 in 1991. Older retirees who manage to augment their Social Security incomes with investment and pension plans are much better off than the rest of the group.

But the "official" income figures for household income give a false picture of buying power, according to Cheryl Russell of New Strategist Publications and Consulting in Ithaca, New York, and Thomas G. Exter of TGE Demographics, Inc. in Rochester, New York. Russell and Exter go beyond the government's Current Population Survey to calculate the amount of discretionary income a household has.

According to their figures, middle-aged shoppers (people between the ages of 45 and 54) are most likely to have discretionary income, but mature shoppers—people aged 55 to 64—have the most discretionary income per household member. Almost 64 percent of all households have discretionary income—$4,300 per household member, according to Russell and Exter. But slightly more than 71 percent of mature consumers (55 to 64), who are for the most part empty nesters, have about $5,400 per capita to spend on nonessentials every year. About 61 percent of households headed by seniors aged 65 to 74 have "a little something extra"—about $4,750 per capita per year. And almost 57 percent of households headed by people aged 75 and older have discretionary income amounting to $4,300 per person per year.

Education has a direct bearing on income and on expenditures of households headed by mature Americans and by seniors. In 1992, the median earnings of men aged 55 to 64 with a high school education was $23,934; those men who had completed a bachelor's degree earned $40,467. And the median earnings of men aged 65 and older with bachelor's degrees was almost twice that of seniors who had only completed high school ($16,333 versus $8,307).

Women aged 55 to 64 who had graduated from high school had a median income of $12,805 in 1992, compared with $21,757 for women that age who held bachelor's degrees. But female seniors aged 65 and older who had only completed high school had higher median incomes ($6,768) than those who had gone on to college and completed bachelor's degrees ($6,593).

In most instances, education is the greatest predictor of income, and most of the highest-paying jobs in this country go to people with college educations. Educated people are also more aware of health and nutrition issues, both of which influence food choices.

With the exception of health care, the total amount spent (per household) increases with years of education, according to Maxine Hammonds-Smith, Joan C. Courtless, and F. N. Schwenk of the U. S. Department of Agriculture's Family Economics Research Group; the way money is spent also varies. Older householders with no high school education spent an average of $2,456 on food in 1990, compared with $4,161 spent by those with a college education. That figure represented only 16 percent of expenditures for the college-educated, compared with 21 percent for those whose schooling stopped in the eighth grade.

Other factors that affect spending on food include marital status and current living arrangements. Women aged 65 and older who live alone are not as well off financially as those who live either with a husband or with other family members. Widowed women have less income and lower expenditures than divorced or never-married women. They also spend a greater percentage of their total expenditures on food (19 percent) than divorced (17 percent) or never-married women (17 percent), according to a study by F. N. Schwenk of the Family Economics Research Group, using data from the 1988 Consumer Expenditure Study.

Even within the mature market, age has a bearing on food expenditures. In 1992, households headed by people between the ages of

65 and 74 spent $2,460 on food at home; those aged 75 years and over spent $1,879.

I I ■ HEALTH AND FITNESS

A 1994 study by *Prevention* magazine and the Food Marketing Institute (FMI) examines the extent to which food shoppers are concerned about health and nutrition. The study also focused on how much shoppers understand the relationship between diet and good health.

The study defined four classes of shoppers based on their understanding of diet and nutritional issues. The first group of shoppers were deemed "Very-Health-Conscious." They have an excellent understanding of diet and nutritional issues, and almost always read the ingredient and nutritional labels when purchasing a food item for the first time. While 13 percent of the total survey group fell into this category, 23 percent of shoppers between the ages of 50 and 64 were very health conscious, as were 9 percent of those aged 65 and older.

"Somewhat-Health-Conscious" shoppers have a good or even excellent understanding of diet and nutritional issues, but are less likely than very health conscious shoppers to read ingredient and nutritional

Label Readers

Almost one in four very health-conscious shoppers are aged 50 to 64.

(percent of adults by class of shopper and age, 1994)

age	all shoppers	very health conscious	somewhat health conscious	not too health conscious	not at all health conscious
18 to 24	9%	6%	5%	14%	17%
25 to 39	37	33	39	35	41
40 to 49	20	25	20	20	12
50 to 64	20	23	23	16	12
65 and older	12	9	11	13	17

Source: Food Marketing Institute and Prevention *magazine*

labels. Forty-five percent of those surveyed were somewhat health conscious, compared with 23 percent of people aged 50 to 64 and 11 percent of those aged 65 and older.

Shoppers who tend to have only a fair or poor understanding of diet and nutritional issues and those who only sometimes read ingredient labels when buying a food item for the first time are defined as "Not-Too-Health-Conscious." While 36 percent of the survey group as a whole fell into this category, 16 percent of respondents between the ages of 50 and 64 and only 13 percent of those aged 65 and older were considered not too health conscious.

Shoppers who have only a fair or poor understanding of diet and nutritional issues and those who hardly ever or never read the label when purchasing a food item for the first time are considered "Not-At-

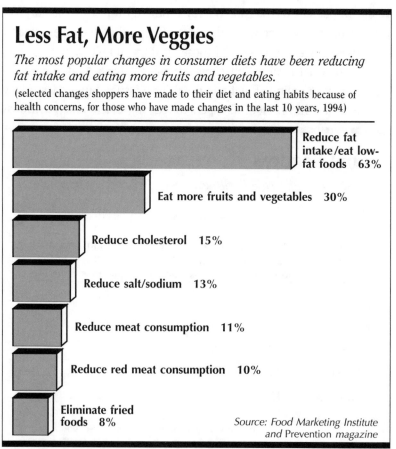

Less Fat, More Veggies

The most popular changes in consumer diets have been reducing fat intake and eating more fruits and vegetables.

(selected changes shoppers have made to their diet and eating habits because of health concerns, for those who have made changes in the last 10 years, 1994)

Reduce fat intake/eat low-fat foods   63%

Eat more fruits and vegetables   30%

Reduce cholesterol   15%

Reduce salt/sodium   13%

Reduce meat consumption   11%

Reduce red meat consumption   10%

Eliminate fried foods   8%

Source: Food Marketing Institute and Prevention *magazine*

All-Health-Conscious." Six percent of those surveyed were not at all health conscious, as were 12 percent of shoppers aged 55 to 64 and 17 percent of those aged 65 and older.

When buying and preparing food, people aged 65 and older are twice as likely to be concerned about limiting salt as people under age 65, according to the 1992 *Prevention*/FMI study. On the other hand, shoppers under age 65 are almost twice as likely to be concerned about limiting fat intake. Both groups are almost equally concerned about eating a generally well-balanced diet.

In general, adults aged 65 and older do not choose to eat more of certain food products specifically for health reasons. While 70 percent of shoppers aged 18 to 64 eat more fruits and vegetables for health reasons than they did three years ago, only 50 percent of older shoppers do, according to the *Prevention*/FMI study. Only 42 percent of the elderly are eating more chicken, while 39 percent have increased their intake of seafood, and 22 percent have decided to eat more yogurt for health reasons.

On the other hand, 58 percent of younger shoppers have increased their intake of chicken, and 45 percent are eating more seafood. Fully 32 percent of younger shoppers are eating more yogurt for health reasons. Consumers have become more aware of the relationship between health and diet. Publicity about the link between diet and heart disease, cancer, high blood pressure, and other debilitating or chronic illnesses has affected the way people shop and eat. Nearly three in five of all shoppers have changed their diet because of health reasons in the last three years, according to the 1992 *Prevention*/FMI study. Shoppers aged 40 to 64, however, are more likely to have done so than those aged 65 or older—64 percent versus 53 percent.

I I ■ HEALTHY SNACKS

Mature consumers are careful about restricting their intake of salt at meal time, but they also watch their salt intake when choosing snack foods. The majority of Americans love salty snacks such as chips, pretzels, and nuts, but the popularity of this type of snack declines as people mature, according to a 1993 study by the Oxford, Mississippi-based Pro-Matura Group, a division of the Institute for Technology Development.

Some 56 percent of Americans over the age of 65 say salty snacks are their favorite between-meal choice, compared with 60 percent of snackers between the ages of 41 and 65. Chips, pretzels, and other salty snack foods were favored by fully 70 percent of people aged 40 and younger. But 18 percent of elderly adults don't snack at all. Only 11 percent of people aged 41 and 65, and less than 3 percent of those aged 40 and younger, avoid snacks. The second most popular snack category overall is fruit, a favorite among 17 percent of elderly, 16 percent of middle-aged, and 12 percent of younger shoppers. Pastries, frozen desserts such as ice cream and yogurt, candy, and other sweets varied little as a favorite choice among the different age groups surveyed. Fewer than five percent of the overall survey group selected these sweet options as their snacks of choice.

As indicated by the ProMatura survey, salty snacks are the junk food of choice for all age groups, and potato chips stand out as the overall favorite in that category. But only 11 percent of heavy eaters of potato chips are aged 65 and older, according to the 1992 Snack Food Association (SNA) *Consumer Snacking Behavior Report.* The most popular salty snack among the elderly are snack nuts. Adults aged 65 and older account for more than 37 percent of heavy eaters—those who snack three or more times every two weeks. And the majority of heavy buyers—households that purchase 5.6 or more pounds of nuts a year—are most likely to be aged 45 to 64.

Other indulgences for the elderly include party mix (some 36 percent of heavy eaters are aged 65 and older) and pork rinds (a favorite evening snack). But the elderly are not great fans of tortilla chips. Less than 7 percent of heavy eaters of tortillas come from this group. Also, they make up only 8 percent of heavy eaters of pretzels and 9 percent of heavy eaters of microwavable popcorn.

I I ■ CONVENIENCE, CLEANLINESS, AND COURTEOUS SERVICE

Elderly shoppers are more loyal to their primary food store than their younger counterparts. In 1994, 24 percent of adult shoppers switched from one primary grocery store to another in the past year, according to the Food Marketing Institute's (FMI) *Trends 94.* But only 12 percent of people aged 65 and older made the big move.

Shoppers aged 18 to 24 are the most fickle, with 46 percent changing stores during the year. Perhaps this tendency reflects the unstable nature of their living situations. Young people are likely to experience life events such as graduation, job relocation, and marriage, which force them to move. The more established the shopper, the more likely he or she is to stick to a favorite store. While 30 percent of people between the ages of 25 and 39 changed stores, 23 percent of those aged 40 to 49 and only 16 percent of shoppers aged 50 to 64 did.

Better or lower prices is the most frequently given reason for switching stores, given by 40 percent of shoppers who switched. But convenient location is the next most important reason for shoppers to switch from one store to another. One-fourth of shoppers surveyed by FMI said they switched stores because of location. Other reasons for changing to a new food store include a wider variety of products (17

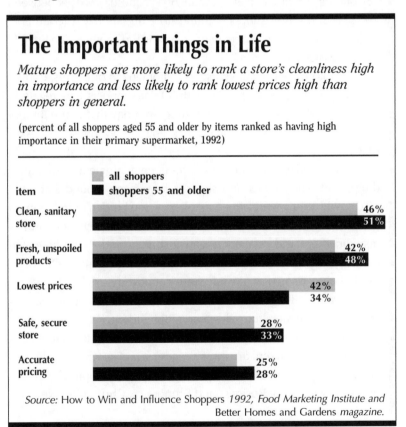

The Important Things in Life

Mature shoppers are more likely to rank a store's cleanliness high in importance and less likely to rank lowest prices high than shoppers in general.

(percent of all shoppers aged 55 and older by items ranked as having high importance in their primary supermarket, 1992)

item	all shoppers	shoppers 55 and older
Clean, sanitary store	46%	51%
Fresh, unspoiled products	42%	48%
Lowest prices	42%	34%
Safe, secure store	28%	33%
Accurate pricing	25%	28%

Source: How to Win and Influence Shoppers *1992, Food Marketing Institute and* Better Homes and Gardens *magazine.*

Senior Discounts

■ ■

The Loeb supermarket in Alexandria, Ontario, has been offering senior citizen discounts on Wednesdays for the last 9 years. Shoppers over the age of 60 get free delivery and a 2.5 percent discount on their purchases. Since a good portion of the store's deliveries are made to older shoppers, the "free Wednesday" incentive frees up store associates on other, more busy days of the week.

"About 20 or 25 percent of the population in Glengarry County is made up of senior citizens," says store manager Michel Ouellet. "By offering a senior citizen discount on Wednesday, we get between 200 and 300 senior shoppers in the store on one day. We are able to deliver the groceries more efficiently, and we can be more flexible on our busier days."

The store does not advertise its senior citizen discounts. Publicity comes instead by word of mouth. Older shoppers congregate in the store mid-week and take their time on a day that is usually not particularly busy. "It's a different scene on Wednesdays," says Ouellet.

Senior citizen discounts on airfare, entertainment, restaurants, drugs, and other goods and services have been around since the 1970s, when they were aimed at relieving the burden of inflation on the elderly. As the mature market became more understood, and as demographers and retailers began to understand its multifaceted makeup, the reason behind discounting began to change. Discovering that older people as a whole were not poverty-stricken but rather affluent and willing to spend, retailers began to use discounts as incentives for generating sales among the elderly.

But as with so many other aspects of marketing to mature consumers, senior citizen discount programs are not universally accepted or successful. A survey published by Lisa D. Spiller, assistant professor, College of Business and Economics, Christopher Newport

University, Newport News, Virginia and Richard A. Hamilton, associate professor, Bloch School of Business and Public Administration, University of Missouri-Kansas, Kansas City, in the *Journal of Consumer Marketing* revealed that only certain groups of older shoppers take advantage of discount programs. Heavy users of senior citizen discounts in general tend to be married and in good or excellent health. They have a high level of education—college or more. They reside in their own homes or in retirement complexes, and they characterize themselves as possessing high levels of life satisfaction.

Light or non-users are more often not married and consider themselves as being in fair or poor health. They are not as educated as the heavy discount users and usually have no more than a high school education. They live in nursing homes or in communities in which their meals and other needs are taken care of, and they describe themselves as having low levels of life satisfaction.

Older married couples who consider themselves to have high levels of life satisfaction and who live independently make use of grocery discount programs. Heavy users are almost three times more likely than the average to take advantage of these offers. People who are in good health are more apt to take advantage of discounts for travel and entertainment, but they do not always do so for necessities like food. And those who rate their life satisfaction highly are more than twice as likely to use grocery discounts than those who feel poorly about themselves.

Targeting appropriate mature segments is the most effective way to market senior discounts. While it may be tempting to assume that all older adults feel the same way about food purchases, even this aspect of mature-market retailing has its own selective clientele.

■   ■   ■

percent), a better meat department (5 percent), a cleaner store (9 percent), employee attitude and knowledge (4 percent), and a better produce department (3 percent).

Shoppers have certain expectations of their food stores. A clean, neat store ranks as "very important" or "somewhat important" for 98 percent of shoppers, including 99 percent of shoppers aged 65 and older. Older shoppers also want a store to have quality produce and a good variety of products. Shoppers aged 65 and older are slightly less likely to demand low prices, perhaps because they use other economizing strategies.

Mature shoppers do not feel strongly that their supermarket must provide 24-hour service in part because they are more flexible about shopping hours, as many people of this age group are retired. Many mature shoppers avoid night driving because of their poorer eyesight and slower reaction time. These shoppers do not particularly care if a store offers 24-hour service. Only 31 percent of people aged 65 and older ranked this attribute as somewhat or very important, compared with almost half of shoppers in general. Stores that offer 24-hour shopping are most popular with adults between the ages of 18 and 24, 65 percent of whom ranked this as an important characteristic. Satisfaction with their primary food store is greatest among elderly consumers. While only one-third of shoppers in general rate their supermarket a 9 or 10 on a scale of 1 to 10, fully half of shoppers aged 65 and older do.

With such strong store loyalty, what can supermarketers do to woo and keep the mature shopper? Customer service is becoming increasingly important as a way of differentiating one store from another, according to a 1991 study by FMI and *Better Homes and Gardens* magazine.

Shoppers favor stores with a high degree of personal service. One in four shoppers aged 55 and older ranks attentive employees among the five most important characteristics of a supermarket, and one in five mature shoppers ranks attentive cashiers that high. These qualities are slightly more important to mature shoppers than they are to shoppers in general. But mature shoppers are not as concerned about careful bagging of groceries. Only 5 percent ranked this quality among the top five most important characteristics, compared with 11 percent of all shoppers. And they are not quite as worried about friendly or courteous service in the store in general as shoppers as a whole (16 percent versus 20 percent).

The shopping habits of mature consumers are reflected in these rankings of supermarket features. Grocery bagging is a good example. Home delivery of groceries—a service that may be more attractive to mature shoppers than to other groups because it would save them a certain amount of effort—obviates the need for careful bagging. As well, mature shoppers head households with fewer individuals and thus may purchase fewer groceries in one shopping trip. Fewer groceries translates into fewer bags, and fewer quibbles about the way in which the groceries are put into those bags.

Mature shoppers may not select friendly or courteous service in the store as an important attribute—but they do point to personal service as an asset. The differentiation between individual service and courteousness in general on the part of store employees may seem insignificant, but it represents the need for marketers to pay attention to mature shoppers' needs on more than a superficial "have a nice day" level. When a mature shopper makes a request or voices a concern, he or she expects a response. Younger shoppers may be satisfied with the concept of friendly or courteous service in general in part because they do not need individual attention quite as often—they can read shelf labels, reach into the back of a dairy case, or spot scanner mistakes without the assistance of store personnel.

Mature shoppers also look for stores that offer fresh and unspoiled products. Forty-eight percent of mature shoppers rate this attribute among the top five, compared with 43 percent of shoppers in general, according to the FMI/*Better Homes and Gardens* survey. But mature shoppers are not necessarily looking for a wide variety of products. While 15 percent of shoppers in general found this to be a significant factor, only 10 percent of mature shoppers ranked it this high. In-store demonstrations and samples are ranked high by 5 percent of mature shoppers, while only 2 percent of the general shopping public gets into taste-testing.

Finally, mature customers are more likely than others to make their feelings known. Eighteen percent of all surveyed customers reported having registered a complaint with their primary supermarket in the past year, but the likelihood of complaining to the store increased with age.

Convenience in the food store means more than personal service. Stores that offer service departments such as delis and fresh-prepared foods appeal to mature shoppers who no longer have large families to feed every day of the week.

❙❙❙ TECHNO-FEAR

Social scientists have for the past decade been studying the way in which consumers react to technological changes. Their research has concluded that older Americans are most likely to resist change in general, and technological change in particular.

In a 1981 study, respondents aged 65 and older were unlikely to have such items as calculators, computers, video recorders, and video games. Other studies have shown that older adults are reluctant to make use of time-saving banking innovations that may involve machine-assisted transactions rather than face-to-face contact with a teller or other bank official.

But is this reluctance a direct result of older Americans' dislike or distrust of technology, or are there other factors that must be considered? "Our surveys have shown that older Americans tend to use technology less. But that does not mean that they are unable to take advantage of innovations," according to Margaret Wylde of the Oxford, Mississippi-based ProMatura Group. "Many of the studies done in the past took technology out of context, without allowing the people using the technology to evaluate the product and its purpose. When technological products are explained clearly and when mature users are allowed to evaluate it, older adults often have better attitudes toward the product than younger ones."

Wylde also suggests that some of the reasons older people do not embrace technological innovations has little to do with the technology itself. "The social situation of older consumers has a lot to do with it," she maintains. "Take ATM machines. Older shoppers may be happier to go into a bank to talk with a teller simply because they have the time to do so, and because they like the social interaction. But if they arrived at a bank after hours, they would use an ATM."

Ergonomically-designed products will attract mature consumers more quickly to new technologies as well. Products that can be used by people whose eyesight is failing and whose dexterity is reduced because of arthritis will find favor with the mature consumer. Sandy Goldman, president of Norcross, Georgia-based ShopperVision, an interactive home-shopping service, points out that the keypad home shoppers use has been specially designed with easy-to-read, extra-large buttons. "We see the mature market as one of our mainstays. For that reason, we designed our keypads with their needs in mind."

But how does this relate to grocery shopping? A 1987 study by Valarie A. Zeithaml of Duke University and Mary C. Gilly of the University of California at Irvine compared the way in which elderly shoppers and those under age 65 reacted to grocery scanners, electronic funds transfers, and automatic teller machines. Just like shoppers in general, the elderly reacted passively to scanners. But elderly consumers were actively enthusiastic about electronic funds transfers. And they rejected automatic teller machines outright, an attitude which may not reflect so much a fear of technology as a different type of socialization.

Supermarkets' scanning technology has obviated the need for item pricing, and most stores with scanners have done away with individual item pricing. Elderly consumers—and indeed many consumers in general—have expressed hesitation about scanners, fearing that the prices recorded on the register tape will not match the unit pricing provided on the shelves.

Unit pricing is also difficult for mature consumers to utilize because the signage is often small and hard to read. Mature shoppers have voiced frustration over trying to read, interpret, and remember prices of specific items. They also have trouble locating the product and matching it to the unit price, since shelf contents often become jumbled over a typical shopping day. Nevertheless, many of the older consumers still patronize stores with scanners. For the most part, they do so for reasons unrelated to the technology. Sixty-three percent of the elderly who shop at stores with scanner technology do so because of the store's convenient location—not because of the scanners. Only 6 percent admitted that they liked scanners, but 5 percent said they liked the detailed register tape that accompanies scanner transactions.

Elderly Americans who shop at supermarkets that have not adopted scanner technology do so primarily because the store happens to be the only one available—not because the store is scanner-free. About 37 percent dislike scanners enough to avoid stores equipped with them. Just 13 percent do not use scanner technology because they dislike the fact that the individual items are not priced separately.

Zeithaml and Gilly cite a number of reasons for the reactions of the mature consumer to technology. In many instances, older consumers are simply not aware of technological advances that may change their shopping patterns. And in fact, the researchers point out that there is a negative relationship between age and the use of specific technologies—the higher the age of the respondent, the less likely he or she had used a specific technology, and the more negative his or her view toward technology in general seems to be.

When studying the reactions of elderly adults to technological change, Zeithaml and Gilly point out that certain socioeconomic, personality, and communication/media variables also affect their choices. Well-educated older adults react more positively to technology and to technological innovation than those who have not attained certain levels of higher education. The researchers also point out that there is a strong relationship between income and technology use and pro-technology attitudes.

Another factor that affects the elderly and their attitude toward technology is their living situation. Mature adults who interact with others, either family members or friends and neighbors in multi-unit dwellings like apartment buildings and retirement communities, are more likely to respond well to technological innovation and make use of such high-tech products as in-store product guides, automatic teller machines, and debit cards. They are able to learn more about such new products and procedures from information garnered from family members, and from others of their same age group, who can provide comparative hands-on experience.

A final influence that can help older shoppers understand and make use of new supermarket technologies is exposure to mass media. Both print and broadcast exposure make the elderly feel less isolated, according to Zeithaml and Gilly. The older shopper will embrace new technologies as long as the benefits of such inventions are communicated to them clearly. They will also discuss the pluses and minuses of new technologies with friends and family before adopting them outright. Education and documentation are the keys to reaching the elderly when it comes to innovations in the technical field.

Americans of all ages and socioeconomic groups are greatly interested in information concerning specific consumer products, according to a 1993 study conducted for the Consumer Federation of America (CFA) and the American Association of Retired Persons (AARP), but the interest varies with age, gender, income, and education. The study asked people to rate their interest in product-related information. Not surprisingly, consumers want details about high-ticket items such as new cars, houses, and health insurance, but only 60 percent of consumers want to be informed in more detail about food purchased at supermarkets, even though food purchases comprise one of the largest percentages of household expenditures.

Older people are more likely to want less information than other groups. While Americans between the ages of 18 and 24 and those aged 65 and older demonstrated the most interest in receiving consumer product information, people aged 25 to 34 and 65 and older had the least interest of any age group.

Limiting the amount of information they obtain about products can affect the choices older consumers make, according to Catherine A. Cole, associate professor of marketing, College of Business Administration, University of Iowa, in Iowa City, and Siva K. Balasubramanian, associate professor of marketing, College of Business Administration, Southern Illinois University at Carbondale. They compared the ways in which younger and older consumers made food purchases based on nutritional information.

When shoppers aged 60 and older were asked to select a cereal based on specific nutritional criteria, they were less likely than younger shoppers to search intensely and select an appropriate product in a supermarket setting. The older consumer needs time to obtain information, read it, and process it in a more controlled environment—at home, for example. A retailer can capitalize on this fact by providing point-of-purchase material that older people can take away with them and read at their leisure. Food stores that provide diet and nutritional information that is accessible and portable—rather than posted in a fixed position in the store—may have more luck in reaching this health-conscious group of consumers. Advertising materials, such as flyers and coupons that are delivered to a mature shopper before he or she actually enters the store will have more impact than unadvertised specials.

In general, though, mature shoppers will take advantage of technology if the product is usable and useful, according to ProMatura's Margaret Wylde. "As long as a technological product is explained in context, and as long as potential mature users can see that the product is user-friendly and has a clear purpose, the mature consumer is no less likely to use it than anyone else."

❙❚❚ MORE SEGMENTS

Understanding the diverse nature of the mature market will shed some light on the issues older Americans consider important. But within the mature market there are more splinter groups and niches than the average supermarket can easily accommodate.

A new approach to segmenting the mature market is to look at attitudes rather than age, race, income, or location. Individual attitudes are more important than any other criteria in defining the behavior patterns of people over the age of 50, according to Carol M. Morgan and Doran J. Levy, authors of *Segmenting the Mature Market.*

Morgan and Levy consider the ways in which older adults react as health consumers and food consumers. Their study differs from the *Prevention* magazine study mentioned above in that they also take into account the ways in which older shoppers regard themselves. In the food consumer category, the authors divide the mature market into three segments—Nutrition Concerned, Fast and Healthy, and Traditional Couponers.

The Nutrition Concerned account for 46 percent of the over-50 set. They believe that what you eat affects how you feel. As shoppers, they stick to their lists and read labels. They also admit that they take advertising into account when buying. Fast and Healthy consumers are also concerned about health and nutrition, but they are more interested in convenience. Microwave ovens and fast foods take precedence over home cooking, which they indulge in only for family gatherings. They represent 38 percent of people aged 50 and older. Traditional Couponers, 16 percent of these older consumers, are not particularly interested in health and nutrition, and they lose little sleep over whether they are consuming too much or too little fiber and fat. When they shop, they are brand conscious and they make the most use of coupons and other incentives.

Another way of looking at the mature market is gerontographic segmentation, a term invented by George P. Moschis of the Center for Mature Consumer Studies at Georgia State University. Gerontographic segmentation takes into account variables that define a person's biophysical, psychological, and social status in life of people aged 55 and older.

Similar to psychographic and lifestyle segmentation, gerontographics focuses exclusively and in much greater detail on the mature market. Using this model, Moschis defines four distinct groups of older adults: Healthy Hermits, Ailing Outgoers, Frail Recluses, and Healthy Indulgers.

Healthy Hermits, the largest of the four groups, represent 38 percent of the elderly market. They are people who are in good health yet relatively withdrawn socially. Healthy Hermits are concerned with day-to-day tasks and are likely to deny their "old age" status. Most Healthy Hermits have experienced major life events—such as retirement, the death of a spouse, or a chronic illness—that have affected their self-esteem and forced them into psychological and social withdrawal. Many of them resent being labeled as "old."

Ailing Outgoers, 34 percent of elderly consumers, are health conscious but in relatively poor physical condition. Although many Ailing Outgoers accept the "old age" label, they are unlikely to change their lifestyle because of chronological age. Health problems and major life events do not affect their self-esteem or lessen their independence, security, or well-being. Because they are a group of active, interested,

Everything Young Is Old Again

Some of the newest products to be pitched to older people are "grown up" versions of goods usually found in the baby-food aisle. The implication that people go full circle and return to their infancy in their old age is a frightening prospect, and marketers must be careful to walk the fine line between the two product classes with diplomacy and sensitivity.

One of the biggest sellers is adult incontinence products, pads or protective undergarments. Marketers stress the freedom these products can give older people. Unfortunately, more often than not, they are placed in the same supermarket aisle as baby diapers. The visible suggestion that adults are no longer "potty trained" may cause shoppers to buy these products in warehouse stores or drug stores, where the chances of being seen with such items in their cart is less likely than in their local grocery store.

Adult incontinence products are marketed by a number of major manufacturers. However, private label products are more than holding their own against the big players in the segment, according to Chicago-based Information Resources, Incorporated. But major manufacturers seem to have the edge in marketing strategy. Many advertise mail-in offers for discretely packaged free samples that are sent directly to the customer's home.

Another product that evokes images of babyhood is a beverage reminiscent of baby formula. Adult nutritional supplements, drinks that contain a balanced dose of protein, carbohydrates, vitamins, and minerals, are aimed at older people who may not be eating nutritionally complete meals. Ross Laboratories' Ensure is advertised as providing "all the nutrition you need every day to help stay healthy, be energetic, and be more active."

Like the ads for baby formula, the product's print ads stress that it is middle-aged adults' responsibility to ensure that the nutritional needs of other family members are met. "When I was a kid, my dad always looked out for me . . . now it's my turn to look out for him," according to a 1994 Ensure print spot featuring a woman and her gray-haired father. The copy for a Gerber baby formula ad is similar—"She's looking to you. For safety. For comfort. For nutrition." Just as with diapers, the line between infancy and old age is blurred.

Other products reformulated for mature audiences stress the differences between children and the elderly. Upjohn's Motrin IB, non-prescription strength ibuprofen, is being marketed in easy-open packages instead of the difficult-to-open child-proof bottles that have been the mainstay of the over-the-counter pharmaceutical industry for years. The new packaging is especially popular with arthritis sufferers, who could not open child-proof containers without assistance.

Some products that used to be for children are now aimed directly at the mature market. St. Joseph's Aspirin for Children (Schering-Plough Corporation) and Bayer Children's Aspirin (Eastman Kodak) are products that baby boomers took when they were children. Medical research has demonstrated that aspirin and children can be a lethal combination because of Reye's syndrome, a rare childhood disease that follows a simple cold or flu. As a result, children's aspirin-based products have been phased out in favor of acetaminophen or ibuprofen formulas.

But medical science gave a new life to children's aspirin when it was discovered that low doses of aspirin taken daily are beneficial to adults with heart problems. Doctors are increasingly suggesting that adults over the age of 50 consume at least 80 milligrams of aspirin a day, according to William Jacott of the American Medical Association. Since many older Americans find it difficult to swallow some forms of aspirin tablets or capsules, the market seemed ripe for Schering-Plough to reintroduce its orange-flavored, chewable form of aspirin. Marketed in the same packaging as the original, complete with the familiar toy soldier, the new chewable aspirin is described as "adult chewable" and is in direct competition with Bayer Children's Aspirin.

As more products are developed to suit the needs of the aging baby boomer generation, "mature boutiques" may find their way into the food stores—one-stop shopping for older customers to get all of the specialized items they need. Presumably these departments could be positioned away from the baby products aisle so that the products needed to ease boomers' second childhood are far away from those that evoke memories of their first.

■ ■ ■

busy consumers, Ailing Outgoers are the opposite of Healthy Hermits.

Frail Recluses are inactive people with chronic ailments who stay isolated and psychologically withdrawn from the world around them. Most Frail Recluses think of themselves as "old people" and are for the most part retired rather than employed. Frail Recluses are very aware of personal security and physical safety. About 15 percent of the elderly fall into this category.

Healthy Indulgers is the smallest of the four segments, accounting for 13 percent of the elderly. Because they have experienced the fewest traumatic moments in life, retirement, chronic illness, or widowhood, they have more in common with middle-aged people than with members of their age group. Healthy Indulgers are socially engaged, active, independent, and relatively wealthy. They pursue leisure activities and involve themselves with community and volunteer activities. What sets them apart from middle-aged Americans is their more secure financial status and settled career. They do not have to prove themselves like many younger people do. They just want to enjoy life.

How do these groups distinguish themselves when it comes to shopping? Healthy Indulgers and Healthy Hermits spend less time shopping and are most cynical about business practices, according to Moschis and Mathur. But Healthy Indulgers are also the group most likely to be attracted to in-store displays, and are willing to pay for lifestyle-enhancing products.

Although they may spend less time shopping than other groups, Healthy Indulgers like to shop and like the independence that shopping for themselves brings. Ailing Outgoers shop selectively because of their physical condition. However, they would take advantage of home delivery of products if such a service was available. Frail Recluses prefer direct marketing, in-home buying, and direct delivery. They would be the least likely of the four segments to spend a great amount of time perusing the aisles of a supercenter.

▮▮ A COMMON THREAD

For all groups, familiarity is an important product or service characteristic. "With age, the human brain loses its ability to evaluate new and unfamiliar stimuli, and older people find it increasingly difficult to use information from their commercial environments," Moschis and Mathur explain.

Since older adults react more slowly and less accurately to sensory information, the best way to reach them is to keep a message simple and familiar, according to Charles D. Schewe, professor of marketing at the University of Massachusetts at Amherst. Older people also lose verbal memory sooner than visual memory — concrete images make the greatest impression.

That may be one reason why so many older Americans remain loyal to a primary food store. Shopping in large supermarkets with more than 16,000 items from which to choose can be bewildering to any shopper. For mature shoppers, changing shopping routines can be daunting. Once a shopping pattern is learned and established, older shoppers can choose the items they desire at a pace that suits them.

To reach the mature market more effectively, retailers may consider providing signage that is legible and placing popular items at eye level, rather than on inaccessible upper or lower shelves. Clearly marked aisles, abundant point-of-purchase information, and available samples and coupons will also make an impression, since these marketing tools have been shown to appeal greatly to the mature consumer.

Understanding the market can net high yields to retailers. Take the example of Bruce Ricks, whose Capital Solutions established a limited partnership to buy a failing shopping center in Laguna Hills, California. Although it was located near a flourishing retirement community, the shopping center was not able to reach its full potential.

By changing the mix of stores—transforming a bowling alley into a rehab center, for example—the mall began to attract older adults in the area. The addition of an adult day care center also boosted traffic. Another draw was the small and accessible supermarket. Only 26,000 square feet, the grocery attracted older shoppers who were unconcerned about extended hours or vast product choices. The convenient size made it a friendly and manageable shopping experience where early-morning shoppers could hang out. Full-size parking spots to accommodate the large American cars preferred by the retirement community dwellers were also appreciated, as was the location. Shoppers could easily be home before dark. By shaping the store to match the needs of its closest constituency—a retirement community—Ricks was able to double his investment in only four years.

❙❙❙ THE MATURITY BOOM

The aging of the baby boomer shopper is of paramount concern to many supermarketers. As boomers move into their fifties and beyond, their shopping styles will change, as will their physical needs and the needs of their households. Marketers are preparing for the changing demographics of their stores brought about by mature boomers.

Boomers are not as concerned about the availability of easy-to-read and accurate shelf tags as mature shoppers, but they rate this a higher concern than baby busters. As boomers begin to age, many supermarketers feel that this attribute will become more important to them, and they are preparing accordingly.

"As the baby boomers age and as the trend to smaller households increases, we're moving more toward smaller packages, single servings, better readability on signage, and more sitdown areas in stores to make shopping more of a social experience," says Gail Omernick, vice president of consumer and governmental affairs for the Copps Corporation of Stevens Point, Wisconsin.

Aging baby boomers will still have some of the attributes they have now when they turn 55. They will still be proactive when it comes to health and nutrition matters, looking for nutritional information and making informed product choices based on health considerations. They will be less brand loyal and more likely to try different foods. And they will still cringe when the store's sound system plays Muzaked versions of Rolling Stones and Beatles hits.

But boomers will also bring with them greater economic health—more baby-boom women will retire on pensions, unlike their older sisters who make up the mature market today. And the increased buying power of women—the majority of mature shoppers—combined with their food wants will be reflected in purchases of exotic foods and new products.

"Maturing baby boomers will make a number of significant demands (on supermarketers)," according to Phil Lempert, senior vice president of Age Wave, an Emeryville, California-based marketing firm. "They clearly state their desires—you can't get away with anything," he maintains. "Stores can become allies with these shoppers by giving them the information they crave." And allying with boomers now will pay off in the future.

CHAPTER 3

Middle-aged Shoppers

money, family, and pandemonium

B ABY BOOMERS didn't invent the supermarket—that was a gift from their mothers. But boomers certainly have changed the way people of all ages shop, eat, and think about food. When baby boomers, people born between 1946 and 1964, moved from their parents' Levittown homes into suburban homes of their own, they brought with them the affluence of post-war economic stability and the expectations of a generation raised to believe that they were always the best.

During the boomers' tenure of as the most prominent generation in the country, supermarkets have undergone massive changes. The small corner store beloved by their grandparents has for the most part been replaced by supermarkets so large that a shopping trip has become an event, not an errand. A typical supermarket now sells some 10,000 different products.

The baby boomer's desire to keep experimenting is the hallmark of this generation. It is reflected in the massive leaps the country has made technologically, socially, and economically during the baby-boom years. And it is even reflected in the day-to-day aspects of the boomers' lives.

In 1993 more than 2,000 new products were introduced. Granted, not all the new products were successful. But even their failures indicate a lot about the baby boom generation, their tastes, their choices, their willingness, and even their eagerness to move from one fad to the next. Marketers have to keep looking ahead to try to predict what boomers will want, even before the boomers know themselves. With a population of 78 million in 1993, the baby boom generation was, is, and for some time will be a force with which to reckon.

But the baby boom generation is fractionalized—by age (younger boomers versus older boomers), by race, and by economics, religion, and political factors. Boomers are not really as homogeneous as we have been led to believe. Marketing to them has never been a "one size fits all" deal. And it will become an even greater challenge as baby boomers age.

The oldest boomers are about to turn 50; their youngest counterparts have just passed 30. But both groups are in a settling-down stage of life. The oldest boomers are almost ready to settle down to retirement, while the youngest are just beginning to settle down to family life. Reaching parents and grandparents of the same generation requires talent, tact, and the ability to change gears quickly.

Boomers have gone from economic boom to bust. They demonstrated through the 1960s, reveled through the 1970s, amassed through the 1980s, and saw their fortunes wane in the early 1990s. While the oldest boomers experienced the full gamut from boom to bust, younger boomers jumped on the bandwagon already in progress. Today, the youngest boomers are experiencing the same difficulties in finding work, the same economic instability, and the same problems in affording homes as people in their twenties.

Older boomers are concerned about their health. Many are beginning to think about retirement. Those who didn't trust anyone over 30 are about to turn 50, and the future is something they want to control as much as possible. Health worries are what motivate most boomers to exercise and to change their eating habits. While not all boomers have become health-food nuts, many are eating more healthy foods and are demanding more information concerning the food choices they make.

But "healthy food" is not food without personality. Boomers are instrumental in the market penetration of multicultural food offerings—from Tex-Mex to Asian and beyond. And boomers have spearheaded the movement to make these formerly exotic foods as common as steak and potatoes—and a lot healthier.

Boomers spend a lot on food—not just for themselves, but also for their families. The hidden power of children and teenagers on boomers' shopping and eating habits will be discussed in Chapter 5. Suffice it to say here that boomer parents are not on their own when they go to the supermarket. Small voices often speak to them, telling them what to put in the basket. And they usually listen.

The boomer generation has shaped the food store, as it has almost every other institution in this country. But when considering the boomers' effect on topics related to food—from shopping to cooking—boomers cannot be discussed in general terms. Special mention must be made of boomer women and the changes their lives have undergone.

Women have always worked outside the home. The mothers of the baby boom generation worked during World War II. Working was acceptable for women before their children were born. Some women even worked all their lives because of economic necessity. And a few successfully managed both families and business. But boomer women were the first to work outside the home in such large numbers. And many have worked at lifelong careers, throughout the time when they had small children at home and even when economic need didn't require them to.

The women's movement moved them from the kitchen to the office, at least for eight hours a day. Instead of being able to spend the day working at home, shopping, cooking, and serving a meal, many working boomer women found themselves in the office for part of the day—but still doing the chores at home, shopping in the evenings or on weekends, and cooking and serving almost every meal. To help them do it all, marketers introduced convenience foods and convenient shopping.

TV dinners, introduced some 30 years ago, and extended food shopping hours, introduced shortly thereafter, made it possible for working women to provide their families with "home-cooked" meals quickly. As women's careers flourished, so too did the convenience-foods industry. And men learned their way around the supermarket and the stove, while children became clever shoppers and gourmet microwavers. Everyone now joins in the shopping, preparing, and serving of meals. Even though boomers are now firmly entrenched in their family years, they are not always able to coordinate. In 1977, 81 percent of families ate dinner together, according to a survey by Roper Starch Worldwide. By 1991, that figure decreased to 73 percent.

The need for convenience will follow boomers into their older years. So too will the need for healthy food, the taste for the exotic, and just about every other characteristic they have demanded. They will just want smaller portions, with larger type on the well-designed and detailed labels.

I I ■ MIDDLE-AGED SPENDING

In 1992, households or consumer units* headed by people aged 35 to 44 spent more on most food products than any other household—primarily because most of these householders have children at home. While the average consumer unit contains only 2.5 people, those headed by someone aged 35 to 44 contain 3.2. And households aged 45 to 54 contain 2.8 people. The figure decreases as the household unit matures—households headed by 55- to 64-year-olds average 2.4

Middle-Aged Consumers

The population aged 35 to 44 will grow 74 percent from 1980 to 2000.

(Middle-aged population, by age, 1980, 1990, and 2000)

age	1980	1990	2000
35 to 44	25,634	37,435	45,123
45 to 54	22,800	24,231	36,170

Source: Bureau of the Census

The Bureau of Labor Statistics' consumer units are not exactly comparable to households as defined by the Bureau of the Census.

members. Those headed by people aged 65 and older average 1.7 members. There are fewer than three members in households of the younger cohorts—households headed by people aged 25 to 34 average 2.8 members, and those headed by people under age 25 average 1.9 members.

In 1992, households aged 35 and 44 spend $3,201 on food at home—21 percent more than the average household. On a per-capita basis, however, middle-aged shoppers do not spend more than other groups in every category. Buying in bulk to feed more mouths is often more economical than buying single-serving portions, and children do not consume as much food in most categories as older people do—although teenagers can give almost any other age group a run for their money. While householders aged 35 to 44 spend an average of $1,000 per person annually on food at home, all households spend $1,056.

Households headed by people aged 35 to 44 spend less per capita on ground beef, bread, poultry, fresh milk and cream, fresh fruits and vegetables, and coffee than older households, but more than households headed by younger adults.

Other categories in which households between the ages of 35 and 44 spend more per capita annually than other households considered by age include mutton, goat, and game ($0.88); frozen fruits and juices (other than orange juice; $3.49); potato chips and other snacks (excluding snack nuts; $26.66); noncarbonated fruit-flavored drinks ($8.81); and other nonalcoholic beverages (excluding coffee, tea, cola, and other carbonated drinks; $6.99). The higher per-capita consumption rates of all of these categories, except mutton, goat, and game, is undoubtedly due to the presence of teenagers in the household, most of whom could happily live on chips and fruit drinks.

Households headed by 35-to-44-year-olds spend $5.39 per capita annually on rice, the same as households headed by 45-to-54-year-olds. On a per-capita basis, households headed by 45-to-54-year-olds outspend all others on cakes and cupcakes ($16.09); ground beef ($37.95); steak ($30.88); sirloin steak ($9.29); cheese ($37.82); miscellaneous foods ($162.34); frozen prepared foods ($33.36); frozen prepared foods other than meals ($23.84); potato chips, nuts, and other snacks ($32.95); sauces and gravies ($18.50); miscellaneous prepared foods ($34.65); and cola ($37.90).

Even though the media have led us to believe that every 40-something woman in America is having a baby, middle-aged households spend much less on baby food than younger adults. But they spend 45 percent more than young shoppers on fresh fruits and vegetables, as well as a wide range of other staples.

On a per-capita basis, middle-aged households spend less for most products than the mature consumer. But middle-aged households are far and away the biggest spenders in most product classes, including meat, poultry, fish and eggs, dairy products, fruits and vegetables, and cereals and bread products.

The Boomer Market Basket

Middle-aged consumers spend more than average on nearly every food item in the market basket.

(average annual household expenditures for selected grocery products, by age, 1992)

product	all households	35 to 44	45 to 54
Fresh fruit	$127.39	$148.47	$139.35
Milk and cream	133.81	164.62	148.22
Fresh vegetables	126.58	142.11	149.09
Poultry	123.10	149.34	142.35
Ground beef	86.66	107.78	106.25
Bread	76.28	86.76	87.56
Potato chips/nuts/snacks	75.64	102.71	92.26
Nonprescription drugs	74.51	79.75	82.35
Toilet paper/tissues	56.62	66.33	68.02
Coffee	38.95	41.30	44.91

Source: Bureau of Labor Statistics, 1992 Consumer Expenditure Survey

I I ■ MIDDLE-AGED DIVERSITY

What middle-aged shoppers buy, how they buy, and where and when they buy, depends on who they are. "Baby boomers are accountants in Boston, unemployed steelworkers in Pittsburgh, coal miners in West

Virginia, ranchers in Wyoming, secretaries in Des Moines, and college professors in North Carolina. There are rich and poor baby boomers, gay and straight, black and white," writes Cheryl Russell, author of *100 Predictions for the Baby Boom.*

Some middle-aged adults are on the cutting edge of styles and trends, and others are content to ride the wave. Marketers can target trendsetters in their middle years, but they should not forget that something one person finds trendy, another finds trivial.

Some trends are real—they can be tracked through surveys and other information-gathering methods. Other trends... aren't. Although they may catch on in the media, there are no hard and fast data to back them up. Such is the case with "cocooning"—the highly touted "lifestyle of the late 1980s," in which jaded yuppies returned to hearth and home, driven by a sense of duty and a taste of economic reality.

Media hype described cocooning as a "return to family values"— for supermarketers, this was supposed to translate into a return to

Spending for 3.2

While the typical household contains fewer than 3 people, middle-aged households have 3 or more—and that's why they're such big spenders.

(thousands of households and average number of persons per household, 1992)

age of household head	total number of consumer units	average number of persons per consumer unit
All	100,019	2.5
Under 25	7,676	1.9
25 to 34	20,763	2.8
35 to 44	21,837	3.2
45 to 54	15,754	2.8
55 to 64	12,225	2.4
65 to 74	11,959	1.8
75 and older	9,804	1.6

Source: Bureau of Labor Statistics, Consumer Expenditure Survey

eating at home. Consumers were said to be shunning restaurants in favor of home cooking, just one of the ways they were allegedly moving back inside the home—to their children, to at-home activities, and after years of living a high-profile consumer lifestyle at restaurants and other away-from-home venues, ranging from country clubs to art galleries and cruises.

But the facts don't quite mirror the fiction. In 1989, Americans spent more than $500 million on food, of which 54 percent was spent on food at home. In 1965, however, that figure was 70 percent. And even though away-from-home food spending began to slow down in the early 1990s, it is still outpacing growth in food-at-home spending. According to the Food Institute's 1994 *Food Retailing Review*, "real" per-capita expenditure for food away from home increased at an annual rate of 1.8 percent in the period between 1970 and 1992, compared with zero growth in "real" at-home food spending.

Spending for food at home and away from home has much to do with the economy. But there are also other factors to take into account, the most important of which is the movement of women into the full-time labor force. Mothers who in a previous incarnation may have spent afternoons cooking are busy at full-time jobs, and the temptation to take the kids to a fast-food joint instead of going home at the end of the day and cooking has a certain attraction. Cocooning may have been a good story, but its trendinesss never caught up with reality.

Marketers waiting for the next trend should pay attention to surveys of trendsetters. A 1990 survey conducted by Ogilvy & Mather looked at consumers aged 18 to 49 who fell into one of three trendsetting categories: Innovators, Early Adopters, and Early Majority. These trendsetters represent half of the general population and give a good indication of where current trends may take us.

The home of the 1990s is taking on a dual role. It is a haven, providing comfort, convenience, and security, and at the same time, providing a way to facilitate activities outside the home. More than 65 percent of trendsetters described their home as a beehive. The beehive is a center of activity for leisure, recreation, eating, socializing, and personal care—and for bringing in goods and services from outside. Another 40 percent of trendsetters described their homes as a "mothership," a kind of electronic cottage. This "window on the world" provides an array of options in home entertainment, information, and goods and services. In contrast, only 29 percent of trendsetters described their home as a cocoon: a shelter in which the family protects itself from the harsh, unfriendly world.

Trendsetters are striving to find ways to improve the quality of their home environment. They are using products that enhance the comfort and security of their homes, especially products that improve the physical environment such as air filters, water filters, and houseplants. They are also "do-it-yourselfers" who improve the comfort of their homes by remodelling and extending living spaces, improving room furnishings, or extending their homes by adding on decks, sun rooms, or porches. Using the home more is an aim of trendsetters. And they are designating areas not only for social and leisure activities, but also for electronic-based enterprises such as home computer use and home entertainment. They use their homes for recreation such as gardening, working out, or playing with their children and pets.

Trendsetters are making a real effort to eat meals at home. More often than not, they hope to eat breakfast and supper at home. Among the reasons they cite for this change are to save money (71 percent), to be with the family (42 percent), to relax (40 percent), for the pleasure of cooking (36 percent), and for convenience (36 percent). For supermarketers, the return to eating at home is very important. Between the social changes of the last decades—women moving into the work force, the time pressures of dual-income families, the number of latchkey children who cook and eat on schedules different from those of their parents—and the technological advances represented by the microwave oven—eating at home will never be the same.

Irma Zandl and Richard Leonard, authors of *Targeting the Trend-setting Consumer,* take a different view of trendsetters. They don't define them by age, gender, race, or marital status. Instead, their trendsetters are united by a commonality of values, which is reflected in their purchase behavior. Trendsetters, or "alphas," as Zandl and Leonard describe them, are well-informed cosmopolitans with highly developed interpersonal communication skills, originality, and independence. They are highly involved in their careers, hobbies, or social causes, and they have a very strong sense of identity and self-sufficiency.

Alpha consumers will be the first to look for gourmet coffee bars in their supermarkets. They caused the rise and fall of clear beer and clear cola. They were the consumers who made Perrier and Grey Poupon household words—and supermarket staples. They brought gourmet foods to supermarket shelves and service departments to the aisles. Their influence will be felt in the grocery store for years to come, as food manufacturers and marketers look to them for the latest "hot" products and services.

▌▌ EATING IN

Trendsetters may want to return to the kitchen, but they're not spending their days simmering, stirring, sautéing, and saucing. Instead, middle-aged chefs are rushing home from their paying jobs and trying to get home-cooked meals on the table as quickly as possible. This does not mean that modern homemakers simply reach in the freezer and grab a frozen entree for the microwave. Although busy people do not have the time to make an entire meal from scratch every single day, appliance manufacturers, supermarketers, and food companies are prepared to meet them half way.

The newest trend to hit the kitchen is "speed scratch," according to John Scroggins, editor of *The Food Channel*. Speed scratch is any method or product intended to save homemakers the time or effort that would normally be required to prepare a meal in the traditional scratch method. This may sound familiar. Forerunners of the 1990s version of speed scratch include cake mixes, macaroni and cheese dinners, and the famous Hamburger Helper.

There are a number of speed scratch appliances and products on the market, and more are predicted. One of the most popular devices currently adored by speed-scratch chefs is the automatic bread maker and associated bread-making kits. Automatic bread makers are electronically programmed appliances with receptacles for liquid and dry ingredients. The unit is loaded and programmed before the bread aficionado goes to bed, and by the time the alarm clock rings in the morning, the bread is ready.

Along with the popularity of the bread-making machine, there has been a flurry of new bread mixes on the market. Maple walnut, cracked wheat, Italian herb, and crusty white bread mixes are among the varieties that have been introduced recently both by small regional companies and by familiar national brands such as Pillsbury.

Other speed scratch items include kits that are comprised of packets of premeasured ingredients which the chef assembles and cooks (frozen fajita kits or packages of frozen vegetables and sauce), or a jar of sauce that a chef pours over browned meat or chicken. Speed scratch also describes recipes that have been simplified for busy cooks. Instead of a dozen of exotic ingredients and two pages of instructions, speed scratch recipes are simple and usually include no more than eight ingredients.

Middle-Aged Trend Setters

Consumers aged 30 to 59 are the best targets for marketing exotic foods.

(percent of adults who have tried selected foods, by age, 1989)

food	total	18 to 29	30 to 44	45 to 59	60 and older
Snake	8%	7%	8%	11%	5%
Eel	11	7	10	15	11
Truffles	11	11	14	12	7
Steak tartare	18	15	21	20	15
Sushi	19	19	23	19	12
Tofu	20	19	25	23	13
Snails	20	17	23	26	15
Tripe	21	13	22	26	25
Octopus/squid	26	24	30	29	18
Caviar	30	23	34	35	29
Quail	32	23	35	36	37
Pig's feet	34	22	34	43	43
Venison	54	45	58	59	56

Source: Roper Starch Worldwide

A recent addition to the speed scratch repertoire has been touch-screen meal-planning kiosks that allow shoppers to choose menus from a wide range of options. The kiosk, marketed by My Menus of Fairfield, Iowa, presents the customer with a shopping list organized by aisles in the store. Along with the recipes—usually an entree, two side dishes, and a dessert—the machine provides the shopper with detailed nutritional information by serving. In some instances, shoppers are also given coupons for the items on their list. Wine suggestions may also be included. The menu machine is currently in 165 stores operated by two different chains in Pennsylvania, Ohio, and California, and plans for expansion are in progress.

The ultimate speed scratch product is still the microwave oven, which was used in 94 percent of American kitchens in 1993. Ten percent of homes boasted more than one of these time-saving appliances, according to a *Parade* magazine survey. Fully 72 percent of those surveyed use their microwaves at least seven times a week. Along with microwaves come microwavable products. Almost two out of three microwave users look for products that have the word "microwavable" on the label, according to *Parade*.

Not all kitchen chefs are microwave maniacs. Some middle-aged adults consider themselves to be gourmet cooks, who prepare gourmet meals for recreation—usually on weekends. Married couples between the ages of 35 and 44 are 38 percent more likely to be into gourmet cooking than average, according to the 1993 *Lifestyle Market Analyst*. Dual-income couples without children, and households with incomes of $75,000 or more are most likely to prepare gourmet meals.

And middle-aged gourmets are more likely than others to try exotic foods. Snake, eel, truffles (the mushroom kind, not the chocolate ones), sushi, octopus, and caviar are more likely to end up on the plates of food daredevils between the ages of 30 and 59 than other groups, according to Roper Starch Worldwide. And households headed by people aged 35 to 44 spend the most per capita on mutton, goat, and game, according to the 1992 Consumer Expenditure Survey.

Middle-aged adults who are interested in fancy foods are also wine connoisseurs. Households headed by people aged 35 to 44 are 17 percent more likely than average to be interested in wine. Single men between the ages of 35 and 44, single women of the same age, married couples, and households with annual incomes above $50,000 are all more likely than average to be oenophiles. By far the biggest wine fanatics are middle-aged people with annual incomes of $100,000 or more. These enthusiasts are more than twice as likely as the average householder to enjoy wine, according to the 1993 *Lifestyle Market Analyst.*

I I ■ AGING HEALTHILY

Middle-aged Americans are the driving force behind America's healthy food revolution. Recent findings by the medical community about the health benefits of certain types of foods have led the way to better eating, and the publicity about health risks associated with high-fat foods and cholesterol have scared some people away from many of the foods they grew up with, including whole milk, butter, ice cream, fatty meats, and eggs. Today's middle-aged adults are concerned not only about their own health, but also about the health of their families.

Eighty percent of shoppers believe good nutrition is important, according to a 1994 study by *Prevention* magazine and the Food Marketing Institute (FMI). When buying foods for the first time, 56 percent of all shoppers almost always read nutritional labels. Another 24 percent read them occasionally. The most conscientious tend to be people in households in which someone is on a restricted diet, older consumers, and more affluent adults.

But many shoppers are reluctant to sacrifice taste for good nutrition. Half (52 percent) of consumers say that nutrition is not more important than taste. And many Americans are indulging. While sales of no-fat salad dressing and mayonnaise, reduced-fat margarine, and low-fat cakes and cookies are increasing, so are sales of premium ice cream, bacon, and salty snacks.

Depending on purchasing patterns, shoppers can be divided into four categories, according to *Prevention*/FMI: Very-Health-Conscious (13 percent), Somewhat-Health-Conscious (45 percent), Not-Too-Health-Conscious (36 percent), and Not-At-All-Health-Conscious (6 percent). Middle-aged consumers (aged 40 to 49) are more likely than average to be found among the Very-Health-Conscious (25 percent) and less likely than average to be found among the Not-At-All-Health-Conscious (12 percent).

Health-conscious shoppers are less likely than others to eat certain high-fat foods. About 19 percent of Very-Health-Conscious shoppers eat no high-fat meat or eggs, compared with 7 percent of Somewhat-Health-Conscious shoppers. About half of shoppers in general eat lean meats (lamb, beef or pork tenderloin, skinless chicken, seafood, or fish) between one and six times a week. An additional 43 percent of shoppers in general eat these products between 7 and 14 times per week, and 5 percent eat them 15 or more times per week. But 40 percent of Very-Health-Conscious shoppers report eating lean meats between one and six times a week, and 44 percent eat them 7 to 14 times per week.

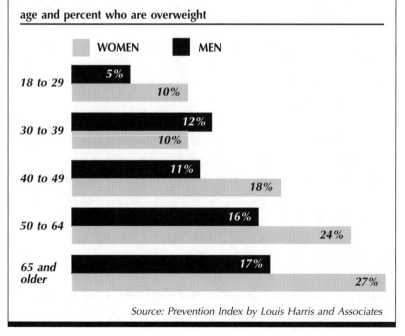

Older and Wider

The older women get, the more likely they are to be at least 20 percent overweight.

(percent of adults who weigh at least 20 percent above their recommended weight range by age and sex, 1992)

age and percent who are overweight

WOMEN   MEN

18 to 29
MEN 5%
WOMEN 10%

30 to 39
MEN 12%
WOMEN 10%

40 to 49
MEN 11%
WOMEN 18%

50 to 64
MEN 16%
WOMEN 24%

65 and older
MEN 17%
WOMEN 27%

Source: Prevention Index by Louis Harris and Associates

Health-conscious shoppers are the most likely to eat adequate amounts of fiber on a regular basis. More than half of the Very-Health-Conscious shoppers and 46 percent of Somewhat-Health-Conscious shoppers eat fruits and vegetables at least 15 times a week. About 30 percent of Very-Health-Conscious shoppers and 24 percent of Some-what-Health-Conscious shoppers eat pasta, whole-grain bread, or brown rice at least that often.

Consumption of all dairy products is higher among more health-conscious shoppers. They consume more 1% milk, skim milk, and yogurt than other groups. But shoppers in general still choose more higher-fat alternatives such as cheese, whole milk, or 2% milk. While 29 percent of the Very-Health-Conscious avoid these fatty foods, 44 percent of the same group eat them about once a day.

Even the most health conscious must indulge sometimes. Fully 71 percent of Americans eat hamburger, sausage, or bacon between one and six times a week, and 70 percent eat eggs that frequently. One-third of shoppers eat butter or margarine 7 to 14 times a week, and mayonnaise and salad dressing one to six times. More than half of the most health-conscious among us eat mayonnaise or salad dressing once a day, and 41 percent eat butter or margarine that frequently. Those who consider themselves Not-Too- or Not-At-All-Health-Conscious are more likely to eat these products more frequently. About half of Americans eat fatty foods only when they are in a hurry, according to the *Prevention* magazine/FMI study, but only 27 percent say they eat fatty foods never or less than once a week.

No matter how much people try to stay away from snack food and desserts, the battle continues. One in four shoppers eats potato chips, corn chips, popcorn, or nuts at least four days a week. Half eat these snack foods at least once a week, and 21 percent eat ice cream, cookies, cake, pies, or other fatty desserts at least four days a week. Forty-seven percent indulge in these diet-busters at least once a week.

Recently, the Food and Drug Administration began requiring nutrition labels to report not only total calories, protein, and vitamins, but also the percent of calories from fat and other, more detailed information. How this new information will affect the consumer is yet to be determined. But the ups and downs of dieting have taken their toll on many people. Faced with a flood of information regarding health, nutrition, vitamins, weight, cholesterol, and fat, it is no wonder that most consumers don't know which end is up. Americans have been trying to change their diets. Six in ten claim that they have made substantial changes in their eating habits over the last ten years. Half have changed the way they eat during the last five years.

The main reason people change the way they eat is concern about weight. But even with increased nutritional awareness, most Americans are overweight. More than two-thirds are over their recommended weight, according to tables from the Metropolitan Life Insurance Company. More men than women are overweight (76 percent versus 66 percent). And while almost 57 percent of younger adults are overweight, fully 79 percent of the over-40 crowd are.

Still, not everyone is on a weight-loss kick. Some people are actively enjoying high-fat foods, according to the *Prevention* magazine/FMI survey. Some pundits see a "deprivation backlash" as former dieters run amok searching for high-fat products in the supermarkets. The number of products bearing "reduced/low calorie" claims on their labels has been shrinking steadily. In 1991, 1,214 new products boasted they had reduced or were low in calories, compared with 609 products in 1993, according to Lynn Dornblaser, publisher of *New Product News*. And while 1,191 new products said that they had reduced or were low in fat in 1991, only 847 made that claim in 1993, possibly in anticipation of new labeling regulations. But, Dornblaser maintains, "There is still a substantial market for health-oriented foods."

"Most of us are in the middle, muddling toward health. We're trying new foods, good and bad; wrestling with new information and old habits; trying to balance health concerns with cost and taste and convenience; struggling to figure out what we can actually live with—in terms of healthful eating—over the long haul," says Tom Dybdahl, director of research for *Prevention* magazine.

❘❚❚ MIDDLE-AGED SNACKERS

Children and their parents—the key players in "middle-aged households"—make up a large percentage of snackers. While kids are more likely to snack at random, their parents are apt to tie snacking to a social event: peanuts at the ball game, chips and hot dogs at a barbecue, and increasingly, salsa and tortilla chips in front of the television.

Potato chips are the most popular salty snack in the country—health considerations aside—and middle-aged adults' consumption of chips has contributed to the immense popularity of that snack product. About 17 percent of heavy eaters of potato chips (people who have four or more servings every two weeks) are between the ages of 35 and 44. This age group constitutes 15 percent of the population in general. At the beginning of the 1990s, household penetration of potato chips reached 80 percent, according to the Alexandria-based Snack Food Association. The heaviest buyers of potato chips are households with five or more members. Heavy chip shoppers are usually between 25 and 54, and, more often than not, they are blue-collar workers.

About 37 percent of heavy potato chip eaters are children, but their parents and parents' friends between the ages of 25 and 54 make up another 38 percent of heavy eaters and 43 percent of the population. Even though children are about 26 percent of all people, they are 37 percent of all heavy chip eaters. People are most apt to eat chips at lunch at home. In fact, more than one-quarter of the chips eaten by Americans are consumed during lunch hour.

Although Americans in general are more aware of health and nutrition, they are still not prepared to give up snack foods, but they are making some concessions. Tortilla chips, another popular snack food, have been reformulated. Many new brands are baked instead of fried. They are presented as a low-fat snack, especially when served with salsa, a spicy Mexican vegetable dip that is usually low in calories. Tortilla chips have been catching up with potato chips when it comes to consumption. At the start of the 1990s, household penetration topped 57 percent. They are now the second most popular snack in every region of the United States, except the Pacific states, where they rank number one.

Heavy buyers of tortilla chips—those households which purchase more than 5 pounds of tortilla chips every year—usually comprise three or more members. Heavy buyers have an annual household income of $27,500 to $44,999—light buyers have a household income between $45,000 and $60,000. The average age of the head of a heavy tortilla chip-buying household is between 25 and 44, and he or she can be either a blue- or white-collar worker. While children and teenagers account for almost half of heavy tortilla chip eaters—48 percent bite into them three or more times every two weeks—adults between the ages of 25 and 54 come in a close second. Four in ten heavy eaters fall into this age group.

Low-fat tortilla chips were first introduced in 1989 by Guiltless Gourmet, an Austin-based company, which instantly created a new niche in the tortilla chip category. When Guiltless Gourmet introduced its first baked tortilla chips, there were 400 regional and national lines of tortilla chips on the market, all of which carried fried snacks. Hitting two of Americans' major eating concerns at once, the new chips (and accompanying cheese and bean dips) were low in fat and made from all-natural ingredients.

Favorite Indulgences

Even though quiet time is the women's favorite indulgence, both desserts and chocolate made the top 10.

(top-ten favorite indulgences of women aged 25 to 54, by age, 1994)

1	Quiet, private time 46%
2	Buying something for myself that I wouldn't ordinarily buy 41%
3	A romantic evening with my partner 31%
4	A hot bath 28%
5	A special meal 23%
6	A manicure, facial, or visit to a hair salon 20%
7	Sex 19%
8	Desserts 18%
9	Chocolate 16%
10	Exercise 12%

Note: respondents chose three favorites

Source: survey commissioned by Continental Baking Company, the makers of Hostess Lights Low Fat Brownies

Another Cup of (Flavored, Gourmet, Estate) Coffee

Before World War II, a pot of coffee sitting on the back of the stove was as ubiquitous a feature of Americana as the pot of tea held so dear by the British. Everyone drank coffee—lots of strong, hot coffee. Housewives had coffee klatches; businessmen took coffee breaks. Wise-cracking diner waitresses served coffee and words of wisdom to truckers, construction workers, and the down-on-their-luck unemployed. No house was complete without a pound or two of Maxwell House.

As baby boomers grew up and their eating habits became more adventuresome, they began to experiment with a wide array of coffee drinks. Trendsetting boomers began to replace their usual canned blend with an occasional pound of freshly ground and freshly roasted gourmet varieties. Instead of just plain coffee, they began to drink Vienna, Italian, and French roasts.

No self-respecting upscale boomer household was without a coffee grinder—usually electric. Some enthusiasts even ground their beans by hand. A popular wedding present of the 1980s was the espresso/cappucino machine. Fancy coffee drinks were de rigueur at the fanciest restaurants and most elegant homes.

The end product is only as good as the beans that go into it. And boomers sought out high quality coffee beans instead of the usual blend of Robustica and Arabica used by the big producers like Procter & Gamble and Maxwell House. The specialty coffee niche was born. Originally a west coast phenomenon, specialty coffees made their way east. Coffee roasters established their own stores and distributed their coffee by mail order throughout the country. And the gourmet whole bean segment began to take off, with whole bean sales increasing about 20 percent annually.

To attract more specialty coffee drinkers, the gourmet coffee sellers began moving into supermarkets, which, except for A&P, almost never sold whole-bean coffee. A&P, while selling products that could be ground fresh in the store, only expanded into gourmet blends in the face of the rising specialty coffee industry. Millstone Coffee, Inc., a whole-bean coffee company established in 1981 in Everett, Washington, markets 70 varieties of gourmet coffee in nearly 5,000 supermarkets in 44 states. Brothers Gourmet Coffees, Inc. of Denver—the largest specialty coffee provider to supermarkets—introduced gourmet coffee bars with operating espresso machines and counter seating in supermarkets in 1994. Each coffee bar is staffed by a professional barista—an expert in the preparation of gourmet coffee drinks who will prepare beverages on the spot for weary grocery shoppers and provide advice for shoppers to brew the perfect cup of coffee at home.

The lure of specialty coffee is reaching beyond the upscale client. "While you do have to have a certain amount of discretionary income to buy coffee that costs $2.50 to $3.50 a cup in a coffee bar, the product is beginning to be adapted by more downscale, even blue-collar, coffee drinkers," says Tom Pirko, president of New York City-based Bevmark, an international food and beverage industry consulting firm. "Like the luxury end of the spirits industry, gourmet coffee is an easy way for people to signal that they are headed in the right direction—upscale, that is."

At current prices of $7 to $10 or more a pound, as opposed to the $3 or $4 a pound for canned supermarket coffee, gourmet

continued...

beans are still beyond the reach of many lower-income coffee drinkers. But national brands such as Folgers, 8 O'Clock, and Maxwell House have begun to try to improve the image of their coffee. Folgers' French roast, for example, is advertised as being "exactly the same" as the coffee consumed by people in France.

"The market is based on images and lifestyles rather than the product itself," says Pirko. "The products sold as espresso and cappucino in the coffee aisles of many supermarkets bear little resemblance to the espresso and cappucino sold in Italy."

Specialty coffees appeal primarily to white, middle-class baby boomers and their parents, who still remember the lure of a good cup of coffee. Generation Xers, according to Pirko, are not particularly big coffee drinkers. They prefer cold and sweet beverages to hot, bitter brews. But the market has found another niche with teenagers.

"There is real activity in this segment," says Pirko. "Kids are beginning to drink coffee again. They especially love specialty or gourmet coffee, which is just different enough for them to want to try. It is not the same old coffee." And the coffee bars springing up in college towns, as well as the presence of specialty coffee areas in supermarkets, makes it easy for them to find a broad array of new types of coffees to try.

■ ■ ■

The product sold nationwide in grocery, natural food, and convenience stores. With 2.5 percent of the dollar volume and 2.1 percent of the market share, Guiltless Gourmet ranked sixth in the category by 1993, according to the A. C. Nielsen Company. And now it is being imitated, both by small companies and by food industry giants, who have jumped on the "baked, not fried" bandwagon. Since Americans are trying to be health conscious, but are reluctant to give up their favorite snack foods, the new subcategory will continue to grow.

Fat is also a concern among snackers of popcorn. In 1994, popcorn sold in movie theaters was the subject of a study by the Center for Science in the Public Interest. Its analysis of movie popcorn revealed that a 7-cup serving of popcorn (the "small" size) contained 20 grams of fat, of which 14 grams were saturated fat. The saturated fat level was about three-quarters of one day's recommended allowance. Bowing to public pressure, most theater owners now serve popcorn prepared with canola, rather than coconut, oil. Keeping popcorn a healthy snack is of great concern to dieters and parents, who rely on the product as a substitute for potato chips and other snacks, most of which are often heavily laden with fat.

Microwave popcorn, now available in flavored and low-fat varieties, was purchased by about 43 percent of American households during 1989-1990, according to the Snack Food Association. It is most popular among middle-aged adults, many of whom are dieters. Heavy buyers purchase 4.6 pounds or more of microwave popcorn per year. These households tend to have three or more people, and they are somewhat upscale, with annual incomes between $35,000 and $59,000. Heavy buyers are most likely to be between the ages of 35 and 54.

More than 2,000 products in the candy/gum/snack category were introduced in 1993, according to *New Product News*. Among the most popular products in the popcorn category were low salt and low-oil formulations, demonstrating again that consumers' concern about eating healthily has translated into a greater range of alternative products in the supermarket.

The issue of health and snacks is more important to non-snackers than to snackers. Non-snackers, people who do not usually consume snack foods, pay more attention to product labels than snackers, according to the Snack Food Association. In 1990, more non-snackers than snackers said that they always use label information when determining which brand of snack food to buy. They are also more likely to buy low-sodium products, avoid chemical preservatives and artificial colors and flavors, and control calories. One-fourth of non-snackers report going out of their way to buy non-fat foods, compared with just 14 percent of snackers.

Enticing nonusers to try a product such as snack food is a challenge. Nonusers of a product are less likely than users to pay attention to advertising for that product, although advertising that is particularly creative and entertaining may attract their attention," according to David W. Stewart, professor of marketing at the University of Southern California, Los Angeles.

Stewart points out that even if nonusers notice advertising for a product a friend uses, they still will probably not buy the product. And some advertising aimed directly at nonusers is more likely to increase purchasing frequency among current users rather than attract the nonuser. But snack food marketers should take heart knowing that even if they can't entice nonusers, creative advertising can persuade "switchers"—people who have little or no brand loyalty, and who make their purchase decisions based on some other parameters. Price promotion and repetitive advertising is likely to attract switchers, according to Stewart, who encourages advertisers not to place too much stock in nonusers.

But while non-snackers are more health conscious, snackers are more aware of price. Snackers are more likely to shop for bargains, stock up on sale items, and clip and redeem coupons than non-snackers, according to the Snack Food Association. Snackers and non-snackers alike will both try new snack products when they are introduced. While both snackers and non-snackers feel guilty about snacking between meals, snackers are more likely to turn a blind eye to adult between-meal snacking and label the practice as a good idea for kids, whom they feel should snack to maintain energy.

▌▌▌ THE SUPERMARKET EXPERIENCE

Middle-aged shoppers rule the grocery aisles. On average, shoppers in their 40s visit the supermarket an average of 2.3 times a week. In a typical week 17 percent visit three, and 9 percent four, times.

What middle-aged shoppers aged 40 to 49 want is convenience, cleanliness, courtesy, and most of all, value for their dollar. The middle-aged wish list is very close to the requests cited by other age groups. But middle-aged people want more. They are particularly concerned about nutrition and health, and they want their supermarkets to make it easy for them to find the healthful products. They want safe foods and they want to shop in stores that practice safe food handling. They want wholesome products—and expect to be told the truth about food additives and food alterations—from BHT in milk to genetically-altered tomatoes. They want to ask questions and get answers from well-trained, competent store personnel.

People in their 40s look for supermarkets with quality produce and a clean overall appearance. They want high quality meat, low prices, and variety, according to the Food Marketing Institute's *Trends 1994*. They are as likely as others to seek out stores with friendly employees. Fresh seafood and clearly marked expiration dates are important to them. Four in five people aged 40 to 49 want their supermarkets to have in-store bakeries or delis. Two-thirds say it is important for a store to have private-label products. Although many busy middle-aged families like one-stop shopping, 36 percent feel it is important for a supermarket to have an in-store pharmacy, according to the FMI study.

Convenience does not necessarily mean the same thing to middle-aged shoppers as it does to the younger adults. Only 43 percent of people aged 40 to 49 want stores that are open 24 hours a day, and 69 percent want stores that have a good selection of non-food products. Middle-aged shoppers—especially those with children—are more likely to make their major grocery purchases on a Saturday as part of a parent/child outing than to run out at midnight to satisfy a craving. They are also more likely than others to frequent other types of outlets (supercenters, mass merchandisers, and drug stores) for household supplies, heath and beauty care products, and paper products.

In a 1993 study, Cornell University agricultural economists Gene A. German, Gerard F. Hawkes, and Debra J. Perosio found that half of shoppers buy household supplies in supermarkets, compared with 63

...do you have any Grey Poupon?

The best-selling brand of "specialty" mustard in the United States today, Grey Poupon was one of the first gourmet mustards to be introduced to the American consumer. Imported Grey Poupon mustard was originally sold in distinctive earthenware containers; the product today is marketed in 8-ounce glass jars imprinted with the familiar antique-style lettering of the original.

Capitalizing on two trends of the mid-1980s—Americans' interest in gourmet and international cuisine and their quest for low-calorie, low-fat food products—Grey Poupon found a profitable niche in the rapidly expanding upscale food trade. Commanding a 78 percent market share among the Dijon segment in 1992, Grey Poupon is for many Americans the mustard of choice. It goes with everything from the lowly hot dog to the fanciest charcuterie plate. And even in the post-yuppie days of the 1990s, when ostentatious is out, Grey Poupon still controls a large share of the gourmet mustard category, with sales of $44 million in 1993, according to Chicago-based Information Resources, Incorporated.

Developed in the city of Dijon, France in 1777, Grey Poupon mustard, a blend of brown or black mustard seeds, white wine, and herbs, was the brainchild of Monsieur Grey, a British inventor, and Monsieur Poupon, a French businessman. Grey developed a steam-operated machine that automated the mustard-making process. The original Grey Poupon mustard shop still exists in Dijon, but all the Grey Poupon mustard sold in America since 1977 has been manufactured in Oxnard, California.

In the early 1980s, the mustard category was divided into three segments: yellow, spicy brown, and Dijon. As Americans began to experiment with Euro-style foods and eating habits, mustard sales flourished. Grey Poupon Dijon and Country Dijon cornered the

Dijon segment. The company moved into the spicy brown market in 1989 with their launch of Grey Poupon Parisian mustard, a special blend of premium brown and yellow mustard seeds, white wine, spices, and a European-style blend of fine herbs. The mustard, developed especially for sandwiches, was "inspired by the mustards used in the cafés of Paris," according to the RJR Nabisco press release introducing the new line. The appeal to the diet-conscious, Euro-gourmet segment was irresistible.

By the late 1980s and early 1990s, a new mustard segment—flavored mustard—was gaining in popularity with the American public. Supermarket sales of flavored mustards accounted for nearly $22 million of the $232 million prepared mustard category in 1992. Many of the new flavored mustards, such as honey mustard, were manufactured by smaller producers. In 1992, Grey Poupon became the first mainstream brand to aggressively support an entry into this segment.

Three Grey Poupon products, flavored with honey, horseradish, and peppercorns, are packaged in the distinctive eight-ounce Grey Poupon jar. Honey and horseradish mustards account for 79 percent of the flavored mustard segment. By introducing flavored mustards under the Grey Poupon name, the company took advantage of brand recognition to move into that increasingly lucrative area.

Savvy marketing and an ability to capitalize on a demographically driven food trend propelled mustard from a lowly condiment into an exclusive, high-class food "accessory." The arrival in America of nouvelle cuisine—a new French food style that veered away from rich sauces and heavy cream—played on our new interest in light foods. Mustard, especially French Dijon mustard, became a more visible flavor, being recommended as a condiment as well as an ingredient in glazes, sauces, and marinades. Soon, the famous tag line "Pardon me, do you have any Grey Poupon?" made the product a household name.

■ ■ ■

percent who purchase these products in supercenters like Super Kmart and Wal-Mart–Supercenter, and 37 percent who make household supply purchases in mass merchanisers such as Ames and Hills. (People can stop at more than one type of store.) The figures for health- and beauty-care items are even more skewed. While 33 percent of shoppers typically buy shampoo, deodorant, cosmetics, and toiletries in supermarkets, 61 percent typically shop at supercenters for these products, and 38 percent make these types of purchases in drug stores.

❚❚ FROM BOOM TO BUST

The picture of the typical supermarket, boomer style, will change as baby busters, the young adults of today, move into *their* middle-aged years. Population projections suggest that households comprised of married couples with children under 18 living at home—the "core" of the current middle-aged population—will decline by 1 million over the next 20 years. And the American population growth in general is slowing as well—over the next two decades, the country's population will increase at an average annual rate of 1.0 percent a year—1.3 percent per year for households.

Marketing tactics have to change to suit the new population forecast realities. Marketers are beginning to turn away from mass marketing to target marketing—aiming to increase their share of each customer's total spending, rather than increasing the number of spenders.

There are a number of ways food retailers can increase their share of the dwindling pie, according to Judith Waldrop, research editor of *American Demographics.* Finding a fast-growing niche to target is one tactic. For supermarketers, that may mean having a broader selection of products that appeal to the Hispanic population, which is increasing at a faster rate than the population as a whole.

But not all supermarkets are located in areas with significant Hispanic populations. Retailers should look at the demographics of their client base to determine which sub-segment to target. Areas that are experiencing an influx of families with small children, those that are seeing an increase in the number of mature shoppers, and those in which patterns of socioeconomic, ethnic, or religious growth can be identified require an update in marketing practices.

Other suggestions for succeeding in periods of slow growth include making customer service a priority, setting a fair price, improving customer retention, and creating incentives to buy.

Advertising in a period of slow growth also requires some new thinking. There are four different consumer groups in a slow-growth market—nonusers, loyals, switchers, and emergents—according to David Stewart, professor of marketing at the University of Southern California, Los Angeles. Stewart maintains that it is more difficult to advertise in a period of slow growth, and that advertisers face a challenge, especially if they aim to recruit nonusers, rather than capture fickle switchers or appeal to emergents. While food retailers may have an advantage over marketers of other goods and services—since they can use a number of strategies such as price competition or increased services—they should still be aware of the changes that occur when markets begin to mature.

Baby busters are people born between 1965 and 1976. As they become middle-aged, they will make an impact on supermarkets. Many of the programs that were put in place to appeal to middle-aged boomers will continue to flourish because they will also be desired by maturing busters. New programs and products will also find their niche.

The features young people look for in supermarkets reflect their lifestyles. They want 24-hour service, an abundance of private labels or store brands, a store with solid environmental programs, and one with a wide selection of products. As busters age, they will continue to look for these "pluses." People who grew up with the convenience of 24-hour service will continue to depend on it, even when they settle down with families of their own. And environmentally conscious baby busters will enthusiastically teach their children about the need for ecologically sound packaging and processes.

There are some things that will change, however. For one, busters will become more interested in cooking. While many young adults have never separated an egg or made a pâté, busters have been on their own in the kitchen for many years. They know their way to the microwave, and they certainly know enough kitchen guerrilla tactics to ensure that they never starve to death.

As busters grow up, they will want to learn more about food preparation. Those who are setting up house independently for the first time will want to—occasionally, anyway—have a dinner party for friends. They will want to impress a date or reward a spouse with a home-cooked meal. And they will want to give their own children something they never had—a chance to bake cookies or frost a cake with Mom on a rainy afternoon.

Busters will also rely more on technology when it comes to food shopping. They have been brought up in the age of scanners—few probably remember life without UPC symbols. And they will continue to look for food outlets that make use of the latest technology. Stores with scanners, those that accept credit or debit cards, and those that provide such technological innovations such as checkout coupons and "clipless coupons" will attract young adults and keep them coming back as they grow up.

Even in middle age, busters will never abandon the supermarket. But they will look to food emporia to provide more than food. They will want a wide array of services under one roof, and they will be more likely to shop at a store that is as much a "food theme park" as it is grocery store. The retailer who can make food shopping fun will have the competitive edge.

CHAPTER 4

Young Adults
new customers/new foods

"WHAT'S WRONG with the young people of today?" That age-old lament has described adults between the ages of 18 and 30 for more generations than anyone could have thought possible. But marketers are beginning to realize that the young people of today become the middle-aged consumers of tomorrow. Instead of complaining about them, it is time to take a closer look at where young adults are now, and where they will be in ten or fifteen years.

Today's young adults were raised by working parents. They are used to fending for themselves. Both young men and women have been preparing their own snacks, lunches, and even dinners since they were teens, or even younger. They are able to find their way around a kitchen—at least on the well-worn route between the fridge and the microwave. They are also able to shop for groceries by themselves, and by the time they are in their late teens and early twenties, many young people are making informed food choices for themselves or for a whole family.

But most young people are also setting out on their own for the first time—whether to college or to the job market. In many ways, they are left to their own devices. No longer shopping from a list prepared by Mom, a young supermarket consumer must make his or her own choices. And marketers know that capturing the loyalty of this emerging market can pay off in shopping loyalty for years to come.

The American Management Association reports that 65 percent of the average company's business comes from current satisfied customers. Getting the substantial population of young Americans interested in a product when they are in their 20s spells at least 40 or 50 more years of customer loyalty. That's a worthy investment.

"Even in a slowly growing market, some new consumers enter while others leave. The characteristics of these emergent customers vary by product category," explains David W. Stewart, the Robert E. Brooker professor of marketing at the University of Southern California in Los Angeles. According to Stewart, one of the two most important groups for a wide range of consumer products is young people.

In order to attract young people, and to build up brand equity with them, Stewart suggests advertising to create awareness of a product, and to build brand image. Advertisements should create a sense of identity with the product and reinforce trial and preference.

But building brand loyalty among young consumers may take a little extra effort. Young consumers can be a fickle bunch. They are into new music, new movies, new technologies. And they are on the lookout for new tastes and new food trends—from Pacific Rim to Mediterr-Asian fusion, some young people will try just about anything.

Just about anything... but only as long as it's the latest fad, and only as long as it's not too expensive. Separating a fad from a trend is a difficult distinction to make, and it is one that benefits best from hindsight. Usually fads have distinctly shorter shelf lives than trends. Fads can also be "subsets" of trends. Nintendo is a trend, while a specific game like Super Mario Brothers is a fad, and marketers must be quick on their feet to distinguish between the two.

While young adults will experiment with food, they may not appear to be as adventuresome as middle-aged consumers. The reason for that may be a matter of money, not taste buds. In a recent Roper Starch survey, 30- to 59-year-olds were more likely to have tried such exotic foods as truffles, venison, or caviar than younger people. But the survey did not include low-budget fun foods like bubble gum, jelly beans, or fancy chocolate-bar confections.

And even though there are young adults who will try chocolate-covered jalapeños, there are those who are still caught in the "giant soda and burger" slump—for these young people, nutritional eating and adventuresome forays into the new foods department of the super-market takes a back seat to junk-food feeding.

Some supermarketers are attracting this type of loyalist by provid-ing fast-food-type counters in the food store, with submarine sand-wiches, pizzas, and salads to go. Others have actually joined the fast-food giants in a profitable partnership by turning over part of their stores to take-out giants such as Pizza Hut, Taco Bell, and Subway.

Regardless of how healthy young adults want to be, they have not given up the snacking habits that began while they were children. But their snack habits are more adventuresome than those of their parents and grandparents. Young adults will eat such novelties as blue corn chips and pink beet chips. They will crunch their way through the rain-forest or drink a path through glaciers, all for a taste of something new.

In order to finance their trendsetting ways, young people must, of course, be gainfully employed. And that is one of the greatest challenges facing the post-boom generation. In an economy recovering from a recession, and with a top-heavy line of overqualified boomers taking a shrinking number of white-collar and manufacturing jobs, younger generations are facing a rough time.

Targeting young shoppers in the food store is not always easy. Sometimes the fads change faster than the products marketed in their wake. Still, there are certain fixed young-adult attributes and habits. Fitness and sports are enduring interests. Marketers have found that capitalizing on this aspect of youth can be profitable. Today's young adults' concerns with ecology and the environment should also be long-lasting. And supermarkets that prove themselves to be as eco-wise as their customers can expect a certain loyalty.

Young people today want to be noticed in their own right, not merely as being the generation that followed the boomers. And marketers

Young Adults on the Move

Forty-six percent of young adults between the ages of 18 and 24 switched primary grocery stores between January of 1993 and January of 1994. That's because young adults are a wandering group. People in their early 20s are the most mobile Americans, according to the Bureau of the Census. Fully 35 percent changed their address between 1985 and 1991. Compare this with 17 percent of Americans in general and 5 percent of people aged 65 and older who did so, and it becomes clear that young adults do not like to sit still.

Young adults move for a number of reasons. They go off to college; they go back home; they leave again to find a job; they go back home again; they leave the nest again to marry or for another job opportunity; and so on.

How can a retailer win a young adult's loyalty and keep it? It depends partly on the young person and partly on the retailer. If a young person moves from one home to another in the same town, chances are he or she will remain loyal to the same food store, especially if the store is near the town's greatest young people's asset —their parents. If a young person moves far away from the parental home, whether it is in the same town or in a different locale altogether, a chain store may have a better chance of keeping him or her loyal. Name recognition is big among young adults—just look at their clothing, emblazoned with brand names. A familiar store name will draw them in just as a familiar beer name draws them to a new neighborhood bar.

If a young person moves to an area in which the food stores do not bear the familiar logos of their hometown markets, there are still things that can be done to draw them in. Some food stores in younger areas have become known as social gathering places—even the stores' audio systems are attuned to young adults' musical tastes instead of golden oldies. In order to attract shoppers, other stores offer sales on youth-preferred products, like frozen pizzas and snack foods.

While young adults are mobile on the grand scale—moving from city to city—they are not always as mobile in their day-to-day lives. Big-city young adults often live without cars; they rely instead on public transportation and pedal power to get around. These young adults, driven either by economics or ecology, would be more likely to be loyal to a food store within walking distance of their apartments or to stores that offer home delivery.

When choosing a primary food store, young adults have a number of criteria. Stores that are conveniently located, with competitive prices and a sense of environmental responsibility, are in a good position to attract and keep the lion's share of their local market.

■ ■ ■

must remember that while this group doesn't come close to their parents in size, it does comprise more than 40 million shoppers. William Dunn, author of *The Baby Bust: A Generation Come of Age,* points out that if today's young adults were a country, they would be ranked at number 24—just ahead of South Korea, and fully one-and-one-half times larger than the population of Canada.

And although there has not been a lot of growth among the young consumer crowd, the number of adults under age 30 will begin to grow again as the baby busters are replaced by the baby boomlet. The baby-boomlet generation will begin to assume the position of household heads by the year 2005, at which point the demographic roller coaster will be set for another spin.

||| YOUNG SPENDERS

When considering the spending patterns of young people, a number of factors come into play. First of all, young shoppers—like all other demographic groups—are not a homogeneous collection of spenders. Some are married; some are parents. And some are married parents, with one, two, or even more children. Still others are college students who live and eat on campus (or in off-campus restaurants) for more than half the year.

During the college-vacation months, students may live at home, where they may or may not be expected to pay their share of the weekly food expenses. Or they may spend the summers away from home,

Young Adults

The number of young adults aged 20 to 34 is expected to decrease in the 1990s.

(number of persons aged 20 to 24 and 25 to 34, 1980, 1990, and 2000, in thousands)

age	1980	1990	2000
20 to 24	21,319	19,132	17,947
25 to 34	37,082	43,161	38,237

Source: Bureau of the Census

working at internships or jobs in college towns or large cities. Some may shop for food and pay for it with their own money; others may do the shopping, but their parents foot the bill.

During the 1991 recession, the U.S. jobless rate stood at 6.7 percent, but the rate for 16-to-19-year-olds was 18.6 percent. And for 20-to 24-year-olds, it was 10.8 percent, according to the Bureau of Labor Statistics. The figure dropped to 6.0 percent for workers aged 25 to 34. In 1993, the unemployment rate dropped to 6.8 percent overall. It was 19 percent for job seekers aged 16 to 19 and 10.5 percent for 20-to 24-year-olds. The rate for workers aged 25 to 44 was 6.1 percent. Finding a full-time, well-paying job gets harder and harder for young adults.

With unemployment looming, many young adults today are either delaying their flight from the family nest or returning to it. College students may continue to live at home when school is not in session, and with the high cost of college educations, many young people are opting to live at home while attending two-year schools or community college. And the tough work of finding a permanent job has driven many college gradutes back home. The economic realities of such a move are felt not only in the shopping patterns of the twenty-some-things who continue to depend on parents for food and shelter, but also for their parents, who are feeding a lot more hungry mouths than they may have planned on in their pre-retirement years. But as the economy continues to improve, young people will once again venture forth. They will have more money to spend, and they will be looking for more ways to spend it.

Household size does play a part in accounting for the difference in spending between young adults and the middle-aged. In 1992 there was an average of 3.2 people in a household or "consumer unit"* headed by someone aged 35 to 44, according to the Consumer Expenditure Survey (CE). There were 2.8 when the householder was aged 25 to 34, and only 1.9 when the householder was under age 25.

But young adults spend less than other Americans even on a per-capita basis. Annual per capita expenditures on food at home for households headed by someone under age 25 were $758, according to the

The Bureau of Labor Statistics' consumer units are not exactly comparable to households as defined by the Bureau of the Census.

1992 CE. The per capita expenditure for households aged 25 to 34 was $888. For Americans in general, the annual per capita food bill was $1,057.

Consumer units headed by adults under the age of 25 spend consistently less on food than any other group, but they do not lag too far behind in some staples. Per-capita spending on canned fish like tuna for these young consumers was about $36.50, compared with a national per capita expenditure of $37.00. But spending on roast beef, a considerably more expensive item, was about one-quarter of the national average among young householders. And while these young people spend about the same on pork chops (about $12.80 annually) as the average American, they spend less than half as much on ham ($9.51 annually).

But convenience foods and sodas are a young persons' essentials. Per capita spending on miscellaneous canned and packaged foods—products other than soups, such as canned stews, spaghetti, and other meals—is actually lower among adults under the age of 25 than other

The Young Market Basket

Young adult consumers spend less than average on most food items, with the exception of 25-to-34-year-olds' spending on ground beef.

(average annual household expenditures for selected grocery products, by age, 1992)

product	all households	under 25	25 to 34
Fresh fruit	$127.39	$62.64	$102.52
Milk and cream	133.81	84.37	131.53
Fresh vegetables	126.58	66.68	114.25
Poultry	123.10	72.71	114.23
Ground beef	86.66	54.10	88.56
Bread	76.28	39.20	70.90
Potato chips/nuts/snacks	75.64	49.79	72.70
Nonprescription drugs	74.51	36.35	48.84
Toilet paper/tissues	56.62	21.22	47.07
Coffee	38.95	15.08	27.99

Source: Bureau of Labor Statistics, 1992 Consumer Expenditure Survey

groups, as is per capita spending on carbonated beverages other than cola. And young households spend less per capita than the national average on cake, eggs, frozen meals, and cola. But they still don't eat their vegetables or fruit, spending only about two-thirds the national average.

They do spend money on baby food, though. Households headed by people under age 25 spend $30.17 per year on food for babies and infants, compared with $47.77 for consumers aged 25 to 34. Paying for baby food must stretch the budget for young single parents, many of whom have only one source of income.

Households headed by someone aged 25 to 34 spend more per capita on almost all food products than younger adults do. But their per capita spending is in line with the national average for almost all products. These young adults spend slightly more than the national average on frozen meals, and canned and packaged prepared foods other than soup. They spend more on fruits and vegetables than do people under age 25, but they still lag behind the national averages in both of these "healthy choice" categories.

Americans in general spent more on foods such as frozen dinners, baby foods, condiments, snack foods, and soup in 1991 than they did in 1986. Spending on these items increased 28 percent in that five-year interval. And young adults rely on these convenience products more than older adults, who make things from scratch.

I I YOUNG MARRIEDS

People are marrying later than they used to. The average age for first marriages among men in 1992 was 26.5. For women, it was 24.4. Many are remaining single while they finish their education or while they establish a career. Some wait until they build up a nest egg, finish sowing their wild oats, or simply gain the confidence to find a mate, stay married, and raise a family.

In 1992, 4 percent of married couples with no children of any age were younger than 25, and 3 percent of married couples with children younger than age 18 were under 25. Young adults are more financially strapped than older spenders. In 1992, the median income in a young (under age 25) married-couple household was $22,283.

Couples between the ages of 18 and 25 with one child spend a larger proportion of their total expenditures on food at home (12 percent) than child-free couples the same age (8 percent). The dollar amount spent on food at home is also higher for young couples with children. Child-free young couples spend more money on food away from home (5 percent) than young couples with kids (3 percent), for whom dining out is undoubtedly a luxury, according to a 1992 study by Mark Lino of the Family Economics Research Group and Geraldine Ray of North Carolina A&T University, who based their findings on 1988–89 Consumer Expenditure Survey data. The economic status of older families—those in which the householder is aged 25 to 35 is on a more solid footing. The median income of a married-couple family in this age group was $39,708 in 1992.

Even though these older families have higher incomes, they spent about the same percentage of their expenses on food at home and food away from home as their younger counterparts. In husband-wife families with both spouses aged 18 to 35, 8 percent of total expenditures were allocated for food at home, compared with 11 percent in families with two parents and a baby. For food away from home, families without children spent 5 percent of their total expenditures, compared with 3 percent for families with a baby in 1989, according to studies by Mark Lino of the Family Economics Research Group.

The dollar amount spent by these couples on food at home in 1989 was higher than that of their younger counterparts. Couples with both spouses aged 18 to 25 without children spent an average of $2,022 on food at home; those with a baby spent $2,481. Couples aged 18 to 35 without a baby spent $2,530; those with one baby spent $3,268, according to Lino.

Young couples are forced to be economical when shopping. They will undoubtedly be the ones to take advantage of coupon offers for baby foods, formulas, and other infant-feeding products; they are also the most likely to take advantage of generics—especially in certain expensive categories like diapers and baby wipes. Even young families without children are feeling the squeeze. Young couples shop carefully and keep an eye out for bargains.

I I ■ SINGLE WITH CHILDREN

Single-parent families make up 56 percent of the group designated as "other families" by the Bureau of the Census. This group accounts for 15 percent of all households in the 1990 census. By far the largest group of unmarried parents are mothers, who account for 85 percent of the total. The number of single mothers under age 25 could grow by more than 50 percent between 1990 and 2020, according to projections by *American Demographics*.

In 1990, single mothers under age 25 accounted for just under 12 percent of single-mother households. That figure is expected to jump to just under 16 percent in 2010. And single mothers between the ages of 25 and 34 accounted for just under 40 percent of single-mother families in 1990. By 2010, their share of the total is expected to shrink to 36 percent as the share of younger single mothers grows with the maturing of baby-boomlet women.

In 1992, two-parent households had more than twice the income of single-parent households ($42,140 versus $18,587), according to the Bureau of the Census' Current Population Reports. And single-parent households spent less on average for food at home per person in 1992 than two-parent households spent. According to the 1992 Consumer Expenditures Survey, per capita at-home food spending in a family comprising husband, wife, and children amounted to $987. For families with one parent, the figure was $784. That averages out to a difference of about $4 per week. Young women who head single-parent families are more likely to economize on food than just about any other group.

But single mothers still have to feed their families. What they buy has changed over the past decade, and in many instances, the ways in which their food consumption has changed is very different from that of two-parent households or single households.

A number of studies have examined changes in diet among households headed by single mothers and those of two-parent families. Between 1977–78 and 1987–88, households headed by single mothers decreased their consumption of most food groups, except fruit and vegetable juices and other beverages (colas, other soft drinks), according to a 1993 study by Elizabeth Frazao of the USDA's Economic Research Service. In fact, this group increased its per-person consumption of beverages like soft drinks by 68 percent. Fruit and vegetable juice consumption was up almost 11 percent. On the other hand, consumption of poultry, fish, and shellfish was down almost 3 percent; fresh fruit consumption was down almost 20 percent, and fresh vegetable consumption was down almost 28 percent.

By contrast, two-parent households increased their per capita consumption of beverages by only 29 percent; their per capita consumption of fruit and vegetable juices was up 21 percent. Their per capita consumption of poultry, fish, and shellfish was up almost 23 percent; fresh fruit consumption was down only 2 percent, and fresh vegetable consumption was down by 14 percent.

As more young women have children and raise them alone, this segment that needs nutritious foods the most but can afford them the least will continue to grow. Like their two-parent counterparts, they will be most interested in bargains and store-brand products. This is the group that will look around for the lowest prices on specific products and take advantage of any cents-off coupons.

Keeping their children well-fed and healthy will undoubtedly take precedence over their own food needs. Many young mothers will be satisfied with a quick soda and a bag of corn chips for themselves while ensuring that their children have fresh juice and other healthy snacks. And retailers who can provide both healthy foods and quick snacks at competitive prices will have the edge for this market.

▌▌▌ THRIFTY GOURMETS

Cooking may not be a passion among young people, but it is a necessity. When 18-year-olds set out for college, even those who are on campus meal plans can usually make themselves a quick snack or a meal that at least pays some attention to the food pyramid. But most young men are not ready to trade their workout clothes for aprons. According to the *Lifestyle Market Analyst 1993,* young single men between the ages of 18 and 34 were 20 percent less interested in gourmet cooking and fine foods than Americans in general. They were 17 percent more interested in fine wines than the population as a whole, however, suggesting that perhaps these young men are willing to drink a merlot with potato chips rather than potatoes gratinées.

Young women are more likely to be found in the kitchen. Single women between the ages of 18 and 34 are 24 percent more interested in gourmet cooking and fine foods than Americans in general, according to the *Lifestyle Market Analyst 1993*. The other groups as interested in gourmet cooking are 18-to-34-year-olds with incomes of $50,000 and higher, upper-class 35-to-44-year-olds with incomes greater than $75,000 and married people between the ages of 18 and 34 with no children at home. Young women are also 43 percent more interested in fine wines than average.

Young marrieds aged 18 to 34 are 19 percent more interested in gourmet fare, according to the survey. Many young adults enjoy cooking and are interested in learning more about it, according to baby bust expert William Dunn. Supermarkets could inspire loyalty by offering cooking classes or demonstrations on a weekly or monthly basis to help young adults learn their way around new foods and new techniques.

But even if they are trying to become the next Pierre Franay or Julia Child, young adults are more apt to take a cooking lesson from Jeff Smith, the "Frugal Gourmet." Four in ten shoppers surveyed by the Food Marketing Institute in 1994 claimed to be "heavy economizers"— people who practice five or more economizing measures. But 48 percent of shoppers between the ages of 18 and 24 fall into this category, as do 46 percent of shoppers between the ages of 25 and 39.

The share of heavy economizers falls steadily with age. Forty-three percent of people between the ages of 40 and 49 are heavy economizers. Twenty-eight percent of people between the ages of 50 and 64, and only 24 percent of shoppers aged 65 and older use five or more economizing strategies while at the supermarket.

Adults under age 25 do a number of things to keep their food bills low. They are more likely to use fewer convenience foods (59 percent versus 49 percent of shoppers in general), and they do more advanced planning of meals and menus (54 percent versus 49 percent of shoppers in general). Adults under age 25 also tend to buy larger quantities than shoppers in general (57 percent versus 45 percent).

But not all young adults are heavy economizers, and not all of them take advantage of every money-saving opportunity. While 32 percent of the shopping public sticks to a shopping list, only 24 percent of adults under age 25 do so, perhaps because of spur-of-the-moment shopping patterns inspired by effective point-of-purchase displays. It's also possible that many of these young people simply do not make a list in the first place.

Budgets and Households

Householders under age 40 are 52 percent of heavy economizers.

(percent distribution of heavy economizers, 1994, and percent distribution of all households, 1993, by age of householder)

age	percent of heavy economizers	percent of all households
18 to 24	7.9%	5.2%*
25 to 39	44.5	32.1
40 to 49	24.6	20.4
50 to 64	13.8	20.6
65 and older	9.2	21.7

*age of householder 15 to 24

Source: Food Marketing Institute, Washington, D.C., and Bureau of the Census

|I■ JUNK FOOD/HEALTH FOOD

Young shoppers do read nutrition labels to make informed food-shopping choices, but not as much as older adults. Twenty-seven percent of adults under age 25 say they almost always read ingredient labels when buying a food item for the first time, compared with 53 percent of older shoppers, according to a 1992 survey by *Prevention* magazine and the Food Marketing Institute (FMI). One-third of 18-to-24-year-olds said that they sometimes check out ingredients, as did 30 percent of people aged 25 and older. One-fourth of young adults hardly ever read ingredient labels when making a first-time food purchase, and 15 percent never bother. Only 11 percent of older shoppers hardly ever read the labels, and just 6 percent of this group confess to not reading product labels at all.

When shopping for different types of foods, young adults do not always consider the importance of nutrition as opposed to other criteria. Only 40 percent of adults under 25 considered nutrition a very important attribute when purchasing fruit juice or drinks, compared with 59 percent of older adults, according to the same survey. And young adults put little stock in the nutritional value of other products as well. While 53 percent of people aged 25 and older consider nutrition when purchasing breakfast cereals, only 37 percent of younger adults do. Margarine and cooking oils come in for more careful nutritional scrutiny by young adults. Still, only 32 percent of people under age 25 consider the nutritional value of margarine an important criterion, compared with 47 percent of older shoppers. And only 42 percent of young adults consider nutrition when choosing a cooking oil, as opposed to 56 percent of older shoppers.

In almost all other categories, the numbers are closer. People of all ages are almost equally concerned about the nutritional value of dairy products. Some 54 percent of adults under age 25 and 58 percent of older adults consider nutrition to be very important. But neither group is particularly concerned about nutrition when choosing snack foods. Only 21 percent of young shoppers and 18 percent of older ones see nutrition as an important factor when buying a particular type of chip, popcorn, or candy.

While young adults may like to eat snack food, they don't seem to have a strong preference for any particular type. People between the ages of 18 and 24 do not distinguish themselves as heavy eaters of any specific type of snack food, according to a 1992 survey by the Snack Food Association. In fact, only 5 percent of heavy eaters of potato chips—the overall favorite snack food—fall into this age group, the smallest percentage of all heavy eaters of chips by age. This is also true for heavy eaters of tortilla chips, popcorn (both ready-to-eat and microwave), pretzels, and extruded snacks.

People aged 25 to 34 (some 17 percent of the total population in 1990) account for the largest percentage of heavy eaters of corn chips. Almost 21 percent of people who eat corn chips 3 or more times a week are in this age group. They are also the second largest segment of heavy tortilla-chip eaters (18 percent) and heavy microwave popcorn eaters (15 percent).

Snack food eating habits were also charted according to gender. Young men between the ages of 18 and 24 eat more potato chips, corn chips, ready-to-eat popcorn, snack nuts, and extruded snacks than women of the same age group. These snack food choices, many of which are high in fat, do not appeal to young women as much as pretzels and microwave popcorn. Pretzels are usually low in fat, or even fat free, and the newest types of microwave popcorn are reduced-fat line extensions, both of which appeal to diet-conscious young women. But women are not without their binge-induced foibles. They account for the total heavy consumption of party mix for the age cohort, and they outnumber men as heavy eaters of tortilla chips two to one.

On the other hand, women aged 25 to 34 eat more potato chips, tortilla chips, ready-to-eat and microwave popcorn, pretzels, and extruded snacks than their male counterparts. In fact, they are twice as likely as men to be heavy microwave-popcorn eaters and almost five times as likely to eat a lot of ready-to-eat popcorn.

You Buy, We Snack

While homemakers under the age of 25 are the least likely to be heavy buyers of snacks, one-third of all heavy snackers are younger than 25.

(percent of all homemakers who are heavy buyers of snacks, and percent of all heavy eaters of snacks, by age, 1989-90)

■ under 25   ▦ 35 to 44   ◩ 55 to 64
▨ 25 to 34   ◩ 45 to 54   ☐ 65 and older

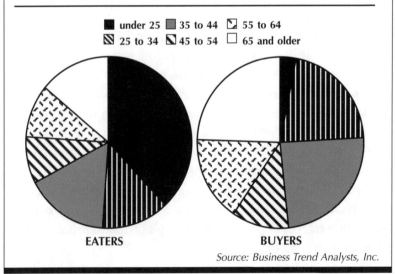

EATERS   BUYERS

Source: Business Trend Analysts, Inc.

Young adults may be the most omnivorous snackers. Yet, even though they are avid snackers, they show no particular allegiance to any specific snack food, according to a survey conducted by Bruskin Goldring for the Continental Baking Company. Some 95 percent of 18- to 24-year-olds indulge their snack food cravings, and the greatest percentage of television snackers belong to this age group, as do the majority of midnight snackers. True to their youthful creed, the highest percentage of those defined as "wacky snackers"—people who crave odd foods—are those between the ages of 25 and 34.

Snacking and guilt are often associated in the minds of overindulgers. But in general, young adults do not feel any great angst in scarfing a few bags of chips here and there. At least 30 percent of Americans have snack guilt, and twice as many women as men (almost 40 percent versus 20 percent) are guilt-ridden as a result of their between-meal indulgences. But when asked to compare the intensity of snack guilt with guilt over other misdeeds, young people scored relatively low. In only three comparisons did 18- to 24-year-olds feel more guilt than older adults about snacking. Seventeen percent considered snacking worse than breaking a date, sixteen percent would feel more guilty about snacking than about lying to a friend, and 15 percent thought it was worse than letting the answering machine answer the phone when they are home.

❙❚ A LOVE/HATE RELATIONSHIP

Want to meet people of the opposite sex? Well, you could try looking in the supermarket. Fully one-third of young women between the ages of 19 and 24 frequent the food store once a week, as do one-fifth of young men in that age group, according to a 1993 consumer panel conducted by the New York City-based Zandl Group. Almost half of young women and one-third of young men make a supermarket appearance 2 to 3 times a month.

Both young men (66 percent) and young women (60 percent) usually dash out to the supermarket to pick up a few essentials, according to the Zandl Group study. But young men are more apt to shop in preparation for a special event (39 percent) than young women (3 percent). The spontaneous grab-and-run shopping habits of young people may explain their pet peeve about shopping—long lines. More than half

Need It Now

For ultimate convenience—especially when you need to just pick up a few things—nothing beats a convenience store. And even though the convenience store usually offers a more limited assortment and higher prices, many consumers are taking advantage of them.

Almost 64 percent of consumers use convenience stores at least once a week, according to a 1992 survey conduced by the Fenton, MO-based Maritz Marketing Research, Inc. Thirty-one percent shop at convenience stores two or three times a week. Men are more likely than women to shop frequently at convenience stores, and younger people frequent them more than older shoppers. Half of convenience store customers are most likely to do their shopping in the evening. Slightly more than 36 percent of people between the ages of 18 and 24, and slightly more than 37 percent of people aged 25 to 34, shop at convenience stores two to three times a week. A further 8 percent of people aged 18 to 24 and 19 percent of aged 25 to 34 shop there once a week. One in five 18- to 24-year-olds stops at a convenience store daily, as do 6 percent of those aged 25 to 34.

People don't shop at convenience stores to save money. Only 3 percent cited price as the primary reason for shopping. The main reason most young people choose convenience store is quick check-out, followed by product selection and convenient location.

Three in ten shoppers aged 25 to 34 cite selection of items as a major lure of convenience stores, as do one in four adults between the ages of 18 and 24. Convenience was a primary reason for shopping for 29 percent of 25- to 34-year-olds and 24 percent of 18- to

24-year-olds. And 23 percent of 25- to 34-year-olds and 27 percent of 18- to 24-year-olds cited quick check out as a major incentive for shopping at a C-store.

What do young adults buy at convenience stores? Usually those essentials that they always seem to run out of at inopportune times—bread, milk, eggs and other staples (most frequently purchased by 26 percent of 18- to 24-year-olds); cola, juice and other beverages (18 percent); and tobacco (10 percent) and automotive products (10 percent).

Convenience stores do not pose a threat to traditional supermarkets, even though their product offerings have increased in recent years. They fill a need—for the odd item that must be picked up quickly, but not necessarily at the lowest price. For emergency convenience, the convenience store is the place to shop; for everyday convenience, shoppers still head for the supermarket.

■ ■ ■

of men and 40 percent of women between the ages of 19 and 24 complain about having to wait in line more than any other supermarket problem.

The on-the-go lifestyle also explains young adults' desire for supermarkets that are open 24 hours a day. Almost two-thirds of adults under age 25 ranked 24-hour service as a very or somewhat important attribute in choosing a primary food store, according to a 1994 survey conducted by the Food Marketing Institute (FMI). Only 45 percent of shoppers in general are this concerned about 24-hour service.

So where do you find all the hip-hop, "gotta" rush young adults? If you want to meet a woman between the ages of 19 and 24, try the produce department. Fully 40 percent of women in this age range rank the fruit and vegetable display as their number one section of the supermarket. You could also try the snack food aisle (favored by 11 percent of young women). The frozen food department or health and beauty aids aisle lure 9 percent each. And the health food department and baking supplies aisle each compel 6 percent of these young women.

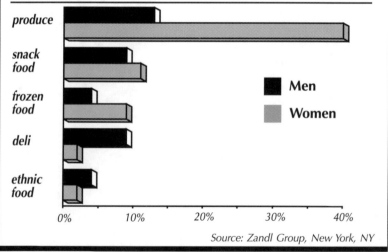

My Favorite Aisle

Women hang out with the fresh veggies, but they're unlikely to meet men there.

(percent of people aged 19 to 24 by selected favorite sections of the supermarket, by sex, 1993)

Men
Women

produce
snack food
frozen food
deli
ethnic food

0%   10%   20%   30%   40%

Source: Zandl Group, New York, NY

However, don't look for women in the meat department. Fully 37 percent listed it as their least favorite section of the supermarket.

Stay away from pet food and feminine hygiene displays if you want to meet young men. These areas tied at 17 percent each as the least favorite section of the supermarket among men aged 19 to 24. Young men frequent the cereal aisle (17 percent), the bakery, produce, and beverage departments (13 percent each), and the snack foods, deli, and dairy departments (9 percent each).

Young shoppers have different expectations about the quality of their supermarket shopping experience than older shoppers. While older shoppers consider attentive cashiers and careful baggers to be important aspects of personal service in the food store, young adults did not give a high ranking to these attributes. They did, however, rank responsiveness to complaints higher than shoppers in general did, according to a 1992 survey conducted for the Food Marketing Institute (FMI) and *Better Homes and Gardens* magazine (BHG). The only other group that ranked responsiveness to complaints highly was adults aged 55 and older.

Young adults are more apt than shoppers in general to want a store to have in-house brands and generics available, according to the FMI/BHG survey. Adults under age 30 are almost four times as likely to want this as shoppers aged 55 and older. But they worry much less about accurate pricing than any other group surveyed—only 19 percent of young adults list this among their top five in-store merchandising characteristics, compared with 25 percent of shoppers in general.

Stores with a wide selection of products and services—from service delis to videos and ATM machines—are popular among young shoppers. When asked which they prefer, a store with several service departments or a smaller store, 73 percent of adults under age 30 went for the store with several departments—slightly more than any other age group, according to a 1991 survey conducted by FMI and BHG.

In general, young adults like stores with great variety, good prices, and quality service, and they give their primary food store a high ranking overall as a place to shop. On a scale of 1 (extremely poor) to 10 (outstanding), young adults ranked their primary food store at 7.4, slightly lower than shoppers in general (who gave their supermarket a rating of 7.9). But young adults are less enamored of their supermarkets in 1994 than they were in 1992, when their satisfaction rating was 7.7, closer to the overall rating of 7.9, according to a 1994 FMI study.

Bigger Is Better

Young adults are more likely than others to prefer larger supermarkets with more departments.

(percent of primary food shoppers who prefer various supermarkets and formats, by age, 1991)

age	several departments	smaller store
under 30	73	24
30 to 44	72	28
45 to 54	71	27
55 and older	63	29

Source: *How Consumers Evaluate Service in Their Supermarket,* Food Marketing Institute *and* Better Homes and Gardens *magazine*

▎▮ ENVIRO-YOUTH

College students are in general more aware of environmental issues than other age groups. Ninety-one percent of people aged 18 to 24 are concerned about the environment and are doing something about it, according to a 1991 Roper CollegeTrack survey. Young adults are involved in recycling and other efforts to clean up the environment. And fully half of students surveyed say that they make brand decisions based on environmental claims on labels or in advertising, compared with 29 percent of all adults.

Young adults think that environmentalists are important and have been a good influence on the country, according to a Times Mirror Center poll conducted in 1992. Eighty-six percent of young adults have a favorable opinion of environmentalists, compared with 80 percent of people between the ages of 35 and 49, and only 52 percent of Americans aged 65 and older. Three-quarters of Americans in general gave environmentalists good grades.

Environmentalism in the supermarket—from organic produce to store-wide recycling programs—has been an important issue for retailers and consumers. As landfills become full, and as the price of dumping has increased dramatically, everything from recycling plastic bags to cutting down on product wrapping is being tried.

Shoppers in general are becoming more aware of how much waste some types of packaging generate. According to a 1994 survey by Roper Starch Worldwide, young people between the ages of 18 and 29 were more likely to suggest that microwaveable trays for frozen dinners should be replaced for environmental reasons than people of any other age group (46 percent, compared with 42 percent of people between the ages of 30 and 44, 45 percent of people between the ages of 45 and 59, and only 37 percent of those aged 60 and older).

More young shoppers are in favor of paper grocery bags than older shoppers. While 67 percent of shoppers between the ages of 18 and 29 thought that paper grocery bags were useful and should remain in use, 61 percent of shoppers between the ages of 30 and 44 agreed. And 66 percent of shoppers aged 45 and older felt the same way.

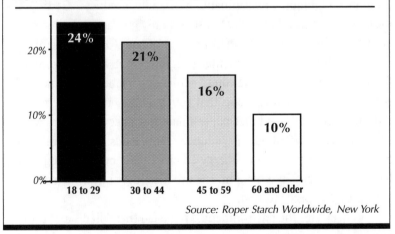

Green Is Better

Young adults are more likely to consider the environment when they make a purchase.

(percent of adults who say that a manufacturer's effort to prevent pollution is important in their purchase decision, by age, 1992)

24%	21%	16%	10%
18 to 29	30 to 44	45 to 59	60 and older

Source: Roper Starch Worldwide, New York

In general, however, the study pointed out that awareness of types of packaging and their potential effects on the environment have spread beyond the younger set. And the efforts of manufacturers to point out that the wrappings on their products are, in fact, recyclable, have also changed the way in which people look at packaging. Now that recycling programs are in place in most parts of the country for many types of plastics, fewer consumers are anxious to change from plastic to other packaging for such products as laundry and dish detergents. But there are still some types of packaging that consumers want to see removed from store shelves—chief among which are aerosol cans for health and beauty products and cleansers.

While just over 11 percent of all shoppers consider a store's environmental policy to be of major importance, 16 percent of young adults under 30 ranked this attribute in the top five, according to a 1992 survey conducted by the Food Marketing Institute and *Better Homes and Gardens* magazine. Compare this with 8 percent of shoppers between the ages of 30 and 44, 8 percent of those aged 45 to 54, and only 7 percent of people aged 55 and older to see how strongly young adults feel about the environment.

Store loyalty can be strengthened even further by a store that is eco-friendly. Young adults are more likely to frequent stores that show as much concern for the environment as they do themselves. Recycling programs, composting, reduction of waste, and re-use of materials are all being tried out by supermarkets. Formal environmental outreach programs highlight environmentally-friendly products. Getting the message to young adults will almost certainly guarantee their support, both of the environmental programs and of the store in general.

It is not just environmental programs, but also environment-friendly products, that bring young adults into a food store. Among the eco-positive supermarket items that young adults buy by the emission-reduced truckload are toilet paper made from recycled pulp, baking soda, non-chlorinated pulp products, organic foods, bottled water, unbleached coffee filters, and energy-efficient light bulbs. Young adults look for the recycled symbol on the products they buy. And marketers are making it easier to find.

Concern for the environment is not a fad that will disappear more quickly—it is a reality that young people are facing with a lot more seriousness than many older Americans. As these young people age, they will still demand products and services that suit their environmental agendas. Marketing to all age groups will have to champion the "three r's" of reduce, reuse, recycle.

I I I FROM BUST TO BOOMLET

Today, the 44 million young people born between 1965 and 1976 are called the Baby Bust, Generation X, or the 13th Generation. But soon this population of young adults will be replaced by the Baby Boomlet or the Echo Boom.

This next wave of young consumers—comprising people born after 1976—will be larger, and probably even more savvy, than the busters who preceded them. According to Bureau of the Census projections, there will be about 44 million "Echo Boom" consumers between the ages of 5 and 23 in the year 2000, and more than 46 million in 2005.

This new generation will be raised by working mothers—much like the people of Generation X. But there will be a difference. Mothers will return to the workplace more quickly, leaving very young children in daycare or with home caregivers. Boomlet children are also more likely to grow up in homes with only one parent—usually their mother, but there will be a lot of single dads out there, too. Single mothers currently account for 85 percent of all single parents, a figure which will only taper off slightly in the next decade. Single fathers, the smallest segment of households, will nonetheless continue to grow in number, at a faster pace than previously seen.

For many people of the boomlet generation, careers will take precedence over marriage—after all, a number of them were raised by parents who had better luck with the former than with the latter. And just like the generations before them, they will have great expectations about success, wealth, and material rewards.

But at the same time, many people of this generation will also be the object of expectations—by boomer parents. Mothers and fathers of the new wave of young adults will be reaching retirement just as their children are beginning to become earners in their own right. The needs of their parents may take away from the income base of many new consumers, who—while earning a decent living—may find it apportioned in more ways than they had originally anticipated.

As food consumers, the next wave of younger Americans will pose many of the same challenges as the current crop of baby busters. But some of those challenges may be intensified—more children will be more independent when it comes to shopping—at an earlier age. They will be entrusted with family food shopping earlier and will *de facto* build some brand loyalty through sheer repetition of weekly shopping lists. Marketers may do well to build brand equity with teenagers now to assure continued loyalty when those kids set out on their own.

Young adults, circa 2005, will have been raised with strong notions regarding the environment and the ways in which marketers do— or don't—respect it. They will undoubtedly make their shopping choices accordingly, looking for packaging that reduces waste, stores that recycle, and products that don't harm the ozone layer.

Health issues are harder to predict. Nutritional information and the importance of low fat diets have been instilled in kids and teens through everything from Barney to school lunch programs. *Prevention* magazine's studies have shown an increased awareness among young people about food and nutrition. These studies, however, point out that in most instances, young people are not as concerned about certain aspects of nutrition and health as older people.

At the same time, smoking has increased among young women and illicit drug use has increased among young people of both sexes, according to recent federal government figures. And people—all people —are getting heavier. Which way will boomleters come down on the issue of shopping for health? Like generations before them, there will undoubtedly be a split between those who only eat healthily and those who don't, with shades of subtlety in between. But it is more likely that the next wave of young people will be more aware of the importance of health and nutrition because they will have so many reminders of the dangers of obesity and poor diet—from the examples of baby boomers who have had to change their own diets to preserve their health.

Marketing to young adults in the future may require some "seeding" now. While marketers may gain insight into this newest generation of consumers by seeing what works with the baby busters, they should also anticipate the differences that will distinguish the Echo Boomlet from their buster forerunners.

CHAPTER 5

Kids and Teens
the hidden influencers

H OW MANY times does a child influence his or her parents' food-shopping choices in a given day? No hard-and-fast figures are available, but even a casual walk around a grocery store provides a host of examples. Parents who bring their children to the store with them are constantly barraged by the whine brigade. With pleas of "Buy me!" "I want!" ringing in their ears, they try to travel quickly through the candy, cookie, or cereal aisle. Teenagers who are asked to do some of the family shopping will inevitably bring home new snack foods or soft drinks to try out, having seen them advertised on television or having sampled them at a friend's house.

Children and teens make specific food choices at every meal—beginning with the morning skirmish between heavily sugared breakfast cereals and more healthful options and continuing at dinner time with the inevitable war of the vegetables. Guerilla activities infiltrate snack times, bagged lunches, and weekend outings.

But not all parent/child discussions about food are acrimonious. As children become more responsible, they have a greater say in the foods they eat. They also are becoming more skillful at preparing their own snacks and meals. Given the independence of their status as "latch-key kids," some children who are left alone or almost alone for periods of time while both parents work have learned to fend for themselves. By their teenage years, they can most definitely take care of their own food needs—from purchase to preparation and consumption.

Kids are also being educated about healthy food choices—some children as young as preschool age have been exposed to the idea of the food pyramid and what constitutes a healthy snack, and not just by their parents and teachers. Television shows like "Barney" and "Sesame Street" and advertisements for healthy foods—milk, yogurt, or fruits for example—drive home the healthy food message.

A broad spectrum of food marketing is aimed directly at children. Parents who think they may have found a safe haven in the healthy snack messages delivered daily by a giant purple dinosaur are not secure. Even if they shield their kids from commercial television, manufacturers can still give their products kid appeal by providing a great deal of point-of-purchase support from life-sized cut-outs or irresistible give-aways. After all, who could pass up Teenage Mutant Ninja Turtles cereal bowls shrink-wrapped to the cereal of the same name?

Other products aimed at children and teenagers are designed to bolster their new-found independence. Microwavable products, from

The Youth Group

Don't look for much change in the youth market during the 1990s.
(the youth population by age, 1980, 1990, and 2000 in thousands)

age	1980	1990	2000
under 5	16,348	18,758	19,431
5 to 9	16,700	18,035	20,531
10 to 14	18,242	17,060	19,972
15 to 19	21,168	17,882	19,819

Source: Bureau of the Census

snacks to entrees, are aimed at the youngest chefs. Pre-cut and pre-measured snacks and luncheon meats in convenient trays also fit into today's young lifestyles.

There were 25 million married-couple families shopping for children under age 18 in 1990. Another 7 million homes are run by single moms and just over 1 million are headed by single dads. Other children receive food and shelter from myriad blended and extended families, living with grandparents or other relatives. The total number of youngsters under the age of 18 was 64 million in 1990. That figure is projected to increase to 69 million by 1995, and to increase again to 73 million by 2005.

There are several reasons for the fluctuations in the number of children from year to year. Women are waiting longer to have their first child, and many women are having fewer children altogether. While the total population of the U.S. is projected to increase by 57 percent between 1990 and 2050, the number of Americans under age 18 will decline from 26 percent of the total population in 1990 to 24 percent in 2050. Fewer children per household means that parents will have more money to spend on each individual child.

Children and teenagers have discretionary income to spend in the supermarket. Their allowance and earnings often go to grocery store purchases, from makeup to personal hygiene products and of course snack foods. Most teens and children do not do the bulk of supermarket spending—but they still exert considerable influence over their parents' spending. Even in families in which the children are too young to speak up, a good percentage of the grocery dollar goes to take care of their needs. Baby foods, formula, diapers, and associated products change the spending pattern of the average family. After the formula, diaper, and baby food phase, the budget is still not out of the woods. Teenagers, especially the voracious appetites of adolescent boys, also have a tremendous impact on grocery bills.

Supermarketers can attract families with children in a number of ways. Low prices and special deals on items that parents buy every week make good sense. Also crucial are amenities like quick check-out lanes, or candy-free check-out lanes for parents who take their young children shopping. Safety features like child restraint belts in the shopping carts

From Blue to Goo

Kids will eat anything, especially if it's guaranteed to drive their parents crazy. A popular kids' food product on the market today is Mad Dog Super Spew Bubble Chew, a type of bubble gum that causes the chewer to foam at the mouth. Then there's Sherman's Super Nauseating Obnoxious Treats (SNOT), a gel-like candy that is dispensed from a plastic nose. Charming. Especially in mixed (adult) company.

Still, children can be convinced to eat foods that have some nutritional value, if the foods also have "something else." That different something may be a wild flavor, a shocking color, or a bizarre texture. Foods with strange flavor combinations designed to appeal just to kids include Nestle's Butterfinger milk and Borden's root-beer milk, two of the biggest players in the flavored milk product category today. Flavored milk drinks are now available in aeseptic packaging, making them convenient to slip into a child's lunch box. And they are gaining in popularity at the same time that the "white milk" industry is declining. White milk sales fell close to one percent in 1993, according to Chicago-based Information Resources Incorporated. At the same time, flavored milk sales were up slightly more than 8 percent.

The new flavored drinks, usually made from 2 percent milk and added flavorings, are competing with the old industry standbys—chocolate, strawberry, and banana. While all flavored milks have about the same nutritional value, the new flavors—which include orange, chocolate cherry, chocolate caramel, and chocolate marshmallow—seem to have caught the fancy of children who may find plain old milk just plain boring.

Nutritionists can't decide which aspect of flavored milk to pick on first. Some condemn the concept of teaching children that milk has to be candy flavored. Others don't mind the flavorings, but chastise the companies for using fat-laden 2 percent milk instead of lower-fat alternatives. Still others see flavored milk as just another nail in the nutrition coffin.

As if the transformation of milk from a healthy food to a sweet snack isn't bad enough, there are the changes in the cereal aisle. It has long been acknowledged that breakfast cereals are a bone of contention between adults and children. Many kids' cereals are heavily sugared and full of artificial ingredients. Manufacturers have been striving to "purify" cereals such as Trix and Froot Loops by using real fruit flavors and reducing the amount of sugar they contain. And cereals that contain fewer artificial ingredients, such as Cheerios and Kix, are heavily advertised for this quality.

The new frontier, however, is to take the "breakfast" out of "breakfast cereal." More than 90 percent of cereal is consumed at breakfast, but marketers are trying to open new avenues for cereal consumption. Advertising spots that show children eating cereal right out of the box, instead of out of bowls, are taking cereal from the realm of breakfast to the world of snack foods, where they compete with traditional products such as pretzels and chips.

The first cereal to be marketed primarily as a snack food is General Mills' Fingos. These sweetened, oversized flakes are advertised as "the cereal meal to eat with your fingers." But in order to ensure that the product is not lost among the snack foods,

continued...

Food for Growing Up

The Cheerios market topped $700 million in 1993, comprising almost 10 percent of the snack cereal market.

(sales of selected children's food products, in millions, percent change in sales 1992-93, and percent share of category, 1993)

product	manufacturer	sales	% change	% share
Selected Snack Cereals (year ending May 23, 1993)				
Cheerios	General Mills	$726.9	3.4%	9.5%
Chex	Ralston Purina	237.8	1.5	3.1
Frosted Mini-Wheats	Kellogg	222.5	16.7	2.9
Crispix	Kellogg	86.3	2.7	1.1
Cracklin' Oat Bran	Kellogg	75.5	-10.2	1.0
100% Natural	Quaker	68.7	1.4	0.9
Cinnamon Mini Buns	Kellogg	51.4	1.9	0.7
Cookie-Crisp	Ralston Purina	43.7	15.0	0.6
Rice Krispie Treats	Kellogg	27.5	*	0.4
Fingos	General Mills	1.7	*	0.0
Flavored Milk Drink Mixes (year ending July 18, 1993)				
Private Label	N/A	46.4	7.0	27.0
Nestle's Quik	Nestle	34.0	6.9	19.8
Borden	Borden	9.7	-4.8	5.6
Hershey	Hershey Foods	6.7	-1.5	3.9
Kemps Moo Jr.'s	Marigold Foods	3.5	12.9	2.0
Selected Blue Foods (year ending July 18, 1993)				
Kool-Aid Great Bluedini	Phillip Morris	18.0	70.7	NA
Hawaiian Punch Fruit Juicy Blue	Procter & Gamble	14.6	80.0	NA
Kool-Aid Kool Bursts Great Bluedinini Juice Drink	Phillip Morris	13.5	155.5	NA
Jell-O Berry Blue gelatin	Phillip Morris	8.1	107.1	NA

* new brand

Source: Information Resources, Inc.

Fingos is sold in the cereal aisle, alongside such cross-over favorites as Ralston Purina's Chex and Cookie-Crisp and Kellogg's Frosted Mini-Wheats, Rice Krispies Treats, and Crispix.

What appeals to a child may not do anything for adults. Kellogg's Rice Krispies Treats, for example, may be way too sweet for adults to eat. But it is not just flavor that turns kids on and adults away. Color, too, can have different effects on different consumers. Such is the case with blue food.

More than 25 blue fruit drinks have been launched since 1989, including Procter & Gamble's Fruit Juicy Blue Hawaiian Punch and Kraft General Food's Great Bluedini Kool-Aid (available in a variety of forms). Blue is the color of choice for Jell-O, which launched its Berry Blue flavor in 1992. It is also popular among candy aficionados, as judged by the popularity of Charms Blue Razz Berry Blow Pops and Totally Blue Razz Hard Candies (both from Tootsie Roll Industries, Inc.).

Blue foods are a novelty item that attract children with their "gross factor." Many of these foods cause hands and tongues to turn (temporarily) a bright shade of blue. But children are fickle consumers, and they will move on quickly to the next fad.

The latest rage are products that are a cross between beverages and gelatin desserts, such as General Mills' Gelooze, sold in plastic squeeze bottles. Launched in 1993, this product is sold as a dessert even though kids seem to enjoy it anytime.

■ ■ ■

are also important. Most parents would agree that a store with other amusements—a tank of live lobsters in the seafood department or a large-screen television in the video rental area—is also a plus.

Youthful Market Basket

Families with school-aged children spend much more than average on many basic food items.

(average annual expenditures for selected grocery products, by age, and presence of kids, 1992)

product	all consumer units	married couple with oldest child under age 6	married couple with oldest child aged 6 to 17	single parent with at least one child under age 18
Fresh fruit	$127.39	$133.91	$173.22	$97.42
Milk and cream	133.81	184.41	210.51	134.39
Fresh vegetables	126.58	132.00	168.98	101.83
Poultry	123.10	136.75	181.90	118.71
Ground beef	86.66	94.32	143.87	101.85
Bread	76.28	81.00	111.03	71.95
Potato chips/nuts/snacks	75.64	96.21	137.01	71.08
Nonprescription drugs	74.51	82.14	70.60	34.99
Toilet paper/tissues	56.62	62.19	75.74	55.52
Coffee	38.95	35.29	51.48	22.08

Source: Bureau of Labor Statistics, 1992 Consumer Expenditure Survey

▌▌▌ SEGMENTING FAMILIES

The world of kids is not homogeneous. Youngsters move through a series of life stages, as infants, toddlers, preschoolers, grade-schoolers, preteens, and teenagers. Each age stage is defined by different needs—and different wants. It is impossible to target all children as a single group.

Even small children have at least some money to spend on their own. But that small amount multiplied by millions of children does add up. When children spend their own money, they buy snacks, toys, and fad items. But children need to be fed and marketers must consider how children influence their parents' spending.

Teens control more money than ever before, and they are frequently independent shoppers. At the same time, parents still have a say over many of the things teens eat. Marketers need to look at the hidden-influencer segment from two perspectives, that of the parent and that of the child.

A profile of the new American family is presented in a study by Simmons Market Research Bureau of New York City, based on 1990 survey data, focusing primarily on parents' attitudes and shopping habits. The study, subtitled "Significant and Diversified Lifestyles," illustrates the way in which the changing demographics of the American population affects consumer goods and services. Of the eight "new American families" described in the study, five focused on families with children or teenagers.

New Mothers are often older mothers. "New Mothers" are women who have had a child in the last year. Sixty-one percent of New Mothers are between the ages of 18 and 29. Another 26 percent are between the ages of 30 and 34, and 13 percent are aged 35 and older. Three out of four New Mothers are married, but 16 percent have never been married, and about 8 percent are divorced, widowed, or separated. About 42 percent of mothers with an infant also have another child at home between the ages of 2 and 5. One in four has a newborn and a child between 6 and 11. Only 12 percent have an older child between the ages of 12 and 14. One in five New Mothers is a college graduate, but half are not currently employed. Of those who are not working, many plan to return to work sometime in the future, although most do not plan to work for at least a year.

The New-Mother family accounts for a disproportionate share of users of baby and children's products, compared with all mothers of children under age 5, according to Simmons. They are 70 percent more likely than other mothers to buy baby soap. They are also heavy purchasers of diaper-rash products, disposable diapers, baby lotion, shampoo, and powder.

Supermarketers who provide a full-service range of infant products—skin-care items, over-the-counter drugs, toys, bottles, and accessories beyond the basics of food, formula, and diapers—will attract these New Mothers. These busy women welcome the convenience of one-stop shopping. They will also feel less compelled to visit discount drug stores or supercenters if the products they need for all aspects of their babies' health and well-being are available at the same outlet as food products for baby and the rest of the brood.

"Sole-Parent" households comprise a sizable minority. Just over 8 percent of U.S. households were headed by a single parent in 1990, and of those 85 percent were headed by single moms. Two out of three Sole Parents are divorced, and 30 percent have never been married. The bulk of Sole-Parent households are headed by people between the ages of 25 and 34 (40 percent). People aged 35 to 44 make up the next largest share (34 percent).

Just over half of Sole-Parent households have two or more children, and 23 percent have three or more children. About half of Sole-Parent households have children between the ages of 6 and 11. Fully 46 percent have older children aged 12 to 17.

Sole Parents are experimental, impulsive, and style conscious, according to Simmons. They are more likely than others to change brands frequently and to buy products on the spur of the moment. But they are also more likely to shop for specials, and this may account for their somewhat erratic product loyalty. Single-parent households are more likely than the average shopper to use microwave food products— especially microwavable hamburgers and cheeseburgers, but also brownies, pasta, french fries, and pizza. Undoubtedly, many of these microwavable meals are being prepared by the children, while mom is at work.

Given the time constraints on Sole Parents, it is no wonder that this group contains a great many avid supporters of convenience foods. They are 85 percent more likely to buy refrigerated or frozen cookie dough, and almost 60 percent more likely to buy frozen or refrigerated pizza crust, than the average householder. They also are more likely to buy toaster pastries, prepackaged prepared entrées, powdered soft drinks, frozen pizzas, and frozen ice cream treats. Marketers who can offer them low prices and a broad array of convenience foods will gain their loyalty.

Seventeen million households in the U.S. include children between the ages of 6 and 11. Comprising 18 percent of all households, "6/11" households usually contain more than one child and two earners. Besides the 6-to-11-year-old, 34 percent of these families have a preschooler and 35 percent have a teenager. Generally, this is a middle income segment. Over half of 6/11 households have annual incomes greater than $30,000, and fully 22 percent are in the $40,000-to-$60,000 range.

The 6/11s know their way around the grocery store. More than half accompany their parents on supermarket shopping trips with some regularity, and fully 15 percent always go to the supermarket with mom or dad. As avid shoppers, 6/11s exert a great deal of influence on their parents' spending. They influence household purchases of products such as breakfast cereals, cookies, candy and gum, and salty snacks. They also have a say in the purchase of boxed macaroni and cheese dinners, corn and tortilla chips, carbonated soft drinks, frozen pizzas, and peanut butter.

Another important segment is the teenage market, according to Simmons. Like the rest of the hidden influencers, teenagers are difficult to track and pin down. Their tastes change regularly with every stage. The youngest teens may still identify with products or characteristics of preteens. Older teens are so close to being adults that their tastes and preferences may overlap with householders in their twenties.

Teenagers are more gender-defined and gender-aware than preteens. The eating and shopping habits of a teenage boy may differ drastically from those of his teenage girlfriend. And they are more capricious than other groups. What's in and what's out is an important distinction made by both boys and girls. The urge to fit in with the group is more important to teens than it is to their younger siblings.

Most teenagers live with two parents, but one in five lives with only one parent. One in three teens lives in a household in which the typical annual income is at least $40,000, but one in three lives in a household in which their parents earn less than $20,000. In families in which both parents work, it is quite common to have a working teenager as well. About one in four teens contributes to the family income.

When asked to define themselves, teenagers say that they are style conscious, trying to keep up with the latest styles and fashions. At the same time, teenagers say that they are economy minded, and that they shop around for bargains or specials. While they say they are careful with spending their money, they also admit to being spontaneous, buying products on the spur of the moment. These descriptions pertain slightly more to older teens (15 to 17 years old) than to younger teens (12 to 14 years old). They also fit the profile of female teens slightly better than males.

Half of teens are brand loyal. But half will settle for another brand if their preferred one is not available. Teens are not particularly experimental in terms of changing brands for novelty or variety. And although they say that they like to be on the cutting edge of style, 42 percent look to their parents for advice when choosing new products.

Teenagers are no strangers to the supermarket, according to the Simmons survey. About 44 percent of teenage girls and almost 36 percent of teenage boys visit the grocery store at least once a month. And 32 percent of teenage girls and 19 percent of teenage boys did major food shopping for their families.

The currently large number of adults aged 35 to 44, so-called "first-wave" boomers, is an important child-oriented segment. Two-thirds of this group are parents, primarily of school-aged and teenaged children. A highly educated and comfortably well-off group, these adults spend a lot of their free time with their children. Forty percent of all PTA members are first-wave boomers and many of their leisure activities—visiting state fairs and playing board games—reflect a devotion to family fun. Older boomers are more likely than other adults to buy any number of products—from VCRs and televisions to home furnishings and wall coverings. And their attention to their children carries through in their supermarket spending.

▌▌▌ FAMILY SPENDING

There's no getting around it—kids are expensive. Parents spend a great deal of their income on children's food, clothing, and care—even in the first few months of an infant's life. And the share of total expenditures for essentials grows as the child does. In 1990 a husband-wife family with an oldest child under the age of 6 devoted 14 percent of the family's expenditures on food, according to the Bureau of Labor Statistics. In a husband-wife family in which the oldest child was between the ages of 6 and 17, food spending accounted for 17 percent of expenses. In a single-parent family, that figure was 19 percent.

The increase in expenses when a family shifts from a two-person unit to a three-person unit, even when that third person is a small baby, can be significant. Young married couples between the ages of 18 and 35 without children spent 8 percent of their total expenditures for food at home in 1989, according to Mark Lino, an economist with the Family Economics Research Group. In families in which there were two parents and a baby, that figure increased to 11 percent, and in families with two parents, a baby, and other children, the figure was 13 percent. On the other hand, the percentage of expenditures for food away from home decreased from 5 percent for child-free couples to 3 percent for families with one or more children.

Mothers who breast-feed save the cost of formula. Children do not usually start solid foods before the age of six months or so, at least according to pediatricians of the 1990s. But as the child grows older, his appetite grows too, and food expenditures increase.

A two-parent household or consumer unit* with the oldest child under the age of 6 spends an average of $3,200 for food at home per year, according to the 1992 Consumer Expenditures Survey (CE). A family in which the oldest child is between the ages of 6 and 17 spends $4,000 per year. And a single-parent family in which at least one child is under the age of 18 spends an average of $2,400 per year.

While children boost the cost of groceries, their presence is not so expensive if you consider food spending on a per-capita basis. On average, 3.5 people live in married-couple households in which the oldest child is under the age of 6, according to the CE. Therefore, the per-capita outlay on food in that family is $913 annually, compared with an average expenditure of $1,057 for consumer units in general. On average, there are more than 4 people in two-parent families in which the oldest child is between the ages of 6 and 17 and the per capita

---

The Bureau of Labor Statistics' consumer units are not exactly comparable to households as defined by the Bureau of the Census.

expenditures on food for that family amount to $956. In single-parent families, there are about 3 people, making the average per capita expenditure for food $785.

Families with children can take advantage of buying food in bulk, which usually works out to be less expensive than buying products in small quantities. In that way, the per capita cost of specific food products is less. For example, annual expenses for bread per capita for all consumer units is $30, but a two-parent family in which the oldest child is between the ages of 6 and 17 spends about $26 per person.

On the other hand, families with children often spend more than other consumer units on products which are favored by children. Ready-to-eat cereal expenditures are about $39 in a married-couple

Older and More Expensive

Even in families with low incomes, teenagers cost nearly twice as much to feed as children under age two.

(estimated annual expenditures on food for the second child in husband-wife families and in single-parent families, by income, 1992)

age of child	low income (under $32,100)	middle income* ($32,100-$51,900)	high income ($51,900 or more)
Husband-wife families			
0 to 2 years old	$690	$870	$1,050
3 to 5	780	1,000	1,270
6 to 8	1,000	1,270	1,520
9 to 11	1,130	1,430	1,710
12 to 14	1,220	1,510	1,870
15 to 17	1,380	1,680	1,970

Single-parent families		**high income ($32,100 or more)**
0 to 2 years old	740	1,110
3 to 5	770	1,210
6 to 8	1,010	1,490
9 to 11	1,080	1,490
12 to 14	1,220	1,800
15 to 17	1,290	1,870

Source: USDA, ARS, Family Economics Research Group,
1993 Expenditures on a Child by Families, 1992.

household in which the oldest child is aged 6 to 17, but only $35 for all consumer units. Potato chips, nuts, and other snacks run about $33 annually for this family, but just $30 in households in general.

Female-headed families spend fewer dollars on the usual food items than two-parent families. But even though the total is less, the percentage of their incomes spent on food at home is greater, according to Mark Lino, an economist with the Family Economics Research Group, and Joanne Guthrie, a nutritionist with the Human Nutrition Information Service. Female-headed households spend an average of $65 per week on food, compared with $107 for two-parent households, 22 percent of total spending versus 13 percent There are significant spending differences between the family types. For all households with children, the largest food expenditures are for bakery and cereal products, milk and dairy products, and miscellaneous prepared foods. But female-headed households spend less per person than two-parent households on these items and in most other categories as well.

I I ■ SPENDING BY KIDS

The other way of segmenting the hidden-influencer market is to focus on the kids themselves. Traditionally, television advertising segments kids into the following groups: aged 2 to 11, and 12 to 17. Sometimes, these groups are further defined as aged 2 to 5 and 6 to 11. These age groupings seem to be, for the most part, arbitrary, according to Horst Stipp, director of social and developmental research at the National Broadcasting Company in New York City. Few market researchers can explain the rationale behind them, except perhaps for the justification of using the age of 6 as an indicator—that is when most children start formal education.

But children are maturing beyond their years. Many 3-year-olds are in formal day care settings, often playing with children older than themselves and learning skills at an earlier age. Just like many children learn to read before they reach kindergarten, make-up and entertainment expenditures begin long before a child reaches the teenage years. Working parents, peer group play, and the influence of early childhood learning programs combine to redefine the relative sophistication levels of today's youth.

Eco-Kids

■ ■ ■ ■ ■ ■ ■ ■ ■ ■

Children are better informed about the environment than their parents and grandparents, according to Harvey Hartman and Gary Lewis of The Hartman Group, an environmental marketing consulting firm in Newport Beach, California. Ecologically minded children are even taking an active role in influencing their parents' behavior.

Children and teenagers have begun to take action in supporting environmental protection programs and actions, both at home and at school. Their primary way to learn about the environment is though school activities, followed by the lessons they learn from television, and the teachings of their parents. Most children participate in one or more environmental activities, among which the most popular are recycling programs.

Manufacturers have reached out to children through television ads which illustrate their recycling practices. And children and teens have contributed to major changes in companies' behavior. Fast food companies have all but done away with hard-shell Styrofoam packaging for their burgers and chicken nuggets. These companies have also begun active recycling programs to convert plastic waste to kids' toys and picnic benches. If children can move a Fortune 500 company to change its way, think of the impact they have on their parents' supermarket choices.

One in three parents have changed their shopping behavior because of what they learned about the environment from their children, according to a 1991 study by the Princeton, New Jersey-based INFOCUS environmental. Fully 17 percent of all households with children have avoided a product they ordinarily would have purchased because they learned something from their children about the product or its packaging. Twenty percent of families purchased a product specifically because they learned about its environmentally beneficial effects from their children.

"Children reported knowing about environmental labeling, and urging their parents to buy green alternatives while shopping. Some of the more aggressive children had taken products out of their mother's shopping cart, returned them to the shelf, and brought back greener alternatives... Children were not above attempting to guilt-trip their parents about non-environmental purchase decisions with statements such as, 'Don't you care about what kind of world you are leaving me?'" said a 1993 Hartman study.

While many of the green-label decisions with respect to the products sold in a supermarket are in the hands of marketers rather than supermarketers, it is still important to understand the influence of children on all aspects of their parents' shopping trips. Some stores have already organized environmental clubs. Other strategies include advertising a store's recycling program or inviting school visits in which the store's relationship to the environment is the focus.

Children are basically optimistic about the chances that people will change their ways and become more aware of environmental issues. They are also not inhibited about expressing their opinions about the environment to their parents—and most parents are willing to listen. Marketers will have to as well.

■ ■ ■

Marketers are rethinking their traditional approaches to splitting up the youth market into manageable segments. And as the market develops and grows, it will not be unusual to see segmenting that refines the age groupings and overlaps them with other significant influencers—gender, ethnicity/race, and economic status.

There are other ways of segmenting children as shoppers. A recent study, based on observation of children and their parents, noted that "young children"—aged 5 and younger—had a number of age-defining attributes as shoppers that distinguished them from "old children"—aged 6 and over.

Among the attributes noted by the author of the 1993 report, Langbourne Rust of Langbourne Rust Research, are the following: First of all, young children ride in or on shopping carts with greater frequency than older children. Young children are also more likely to point at things than older children, even if they are walking, not riding. They are also a lot more likely to get physically involved with a product. While older children may pick up a product and put it in a shopping cart, young children are apt to play with the product, open up the box, eat the product, and get more physically involved than their older siblings.

Parent involvement is another important element. Parents are more likely to be firm when refusing a younger child than an older child. Children between the ages of 6 and 9 show skills in negotiating and are sometimes successful at it; children aged 10 and older get their own way more often. Older children are usually more involved in a shopping trip than younger children, helping to plan the shopping in advance and helping their parents in the food store.

The implications of these observations can be beneficial to marketers and retailers alike. Rust suggests that since it is young children who are most often using the shopping cart as a vehicle or toy, marketers should direct the information on the cart to the child inside. Instead of directing cart advertising to parents, who may not be paying attention, it would be more beneficial to communicate marketing information in such a way that it provides genuine benefits to parents and children.

Rust also suggests that products should be displayed at cart height, especially products targeted at young children. Products for children traditionally have been placed on the lowest shelves, but these are not visible to kids riding in carts.

Since young children tend to point at products, Rust suggests that point-of-purchase material should point back. Producing product advertising that allows children to interact with an image is an excellent marketing tactic. Packaging and products should also be designed to encourage interaction and physical involvement. Activities that use the box as a prop could be very attractive—for example, packages with handles will get children to ask their parents if they may carry the product to the checkout. This marketing tactic was used for many years by manufacturers of animal crackers, who equipped each small box of the product with a string handle so that children could carry them around.

To encourage older children to be helpful members of the "shopping team," Rust suggests that retailers appeal to the positive sides of the shopping experience for both children and their parents. Casting the child as a helper and team player through store incentives or point-of-purchase material can be beneficial.

There are other ways in which children can be made to become more involved in shopping, given their attitudes in the supermarket. Advertisers, retailers, and manufacturers should invest time in observing child-parent shopping teams in order to evolve strategies that appeal to adults and children alike.

Children are an important segment of the shopping community. Their spending power is substantial and increasing. Young children spend a lot of time in the grocery store. And many of them have learned their way around the aisles by the time they're preschoolers, according to a study by James McNeal, professor of marketing at Texas A&M University in College Station, and Chyon-Hwa Yeh, statistical consultant at Procter & Gamble's Sharon Woods Technical Center in Cincinnati, Ohio. Between the age of one month and 8 years, children go through a five-stage process in their education as consumers.

In the first stage, children are introduced to the concept of shopping by their mothers, who take the babies with them on shopping outings. Kids as young as one month old accompany their parents to the store, and about three out of four children have been to the store by the time they're 6 months old. Just under 80 percent of their shopping time is spent in the grocery store at this stage.

Grocery stores play an important role in the next phase, in which children begin to make requests while in stores. They have been conditioned to know that something good comes out of shopping. Many parents use food as a bribe to quiet a fussy baby in the store. Some children begin requesting products as early as 6 or 7 months—but half of children don't begin this stage until age 2.

The third stage of consumer education for kids is the period when children begin to make their own selections. With permission, children may leave the safe haven of the grocery cart and actually choose products themselves. At this point, kids spend about 55 percent of their store time in supermarkets. Although a precocious one-year-old may already be in this stage, half of children are over age 3 before they reach this level.

Children begin to make assisted purchases by the time they are 5 or 6, although some advanced 2-year-olds have mastered this skill. At this stage, children begin to understand the relationship between choosing and purchasing products. With their parents watching, they graduate from passive observer to primary consumers. Slightly less than 20 percent of their time shopping with their parents is spent in the grocery store, but marketers can be sure that with the broad array of kid-specific snacks, cereals, and other food products, there will still be a not inconsiderable amount of kid-merchant interaction.

The final stage is the one in which children make independent purchases. This usually happens when the child is around 8 years old. Parents are loath to let their children go to a store alone—which partly explains the three-year gap between assisted purchases and independent purchases. At this point, only slightly more than 10 percent of a kid's shopping time is spent in a supermarket. The majority of their time is spent in convenience stores, where food purchases can also be made.

By the time they are preschoolers, kids begin to favor mass merchandisers over supermarkets. But convenience stores move into the lead when children become independent buyers, in part because of location. Most children can go to the corner store on foot or by bicycle alone.

In stage 2, just under 80 percent of items purchased at the request of children are food and snack products. But by stage 3, the share of food and snacks drops to about 60 percent. This changes dramatically in stage 4, when children tend to buy toys with the assistance of their parents. Only about 30 percent of assisted purchases are food and snacks. But in stage 5, when children go shopping alone, they choose food and snacks about 65 percent of the time.

On average, children go to the store with their parents two or three times a week. They go to the store once a week on their own. On average, girls go shopping by themselves a little less than once a week, but boys go somewhat more frequently. Parents may be more concerned about letting girls go out by themselves than they are about boys, but girls go shopping with their parents slightly more frequently than boys.

Between 1989 and 1991, the income of children aged 4 to 8 increased 82 percent, according to Texas A&M's James McNeal. He points out this huge increase is especially significant since kids' incomes are almost entirely discretionary. Kids can spend their money any way they want—on video games, toys, sports equipment ... and food.

The income of children aged 4 to 8 increased an average of 113 percent between 1989 and 1991, compared with 45 percent for children between the ages of 9 and 12. That's because parents have come to see their preschoolers and kindergartners as consumers in their own right. Kids are being taught how to be wise savers, and parents are encouraging kids to be more responsible with their money.

In 1991, children saved 40 percent of their income, compared with 31 percent in 1989. That leaves 60 percent to be spent on fun items. Two surveys conducted by McNeal in 1989 and 1991 found that about two-thirds of children's spending concentrated on snacks and playthings. The rest was used for purchasing clothing, outside-the-home entertainment, and miscellaneous other items such as electronics.

The average 4-year-old had almost $4 per week to spend in 1991. The average 12-year-old had $15. While that may not seem to be very much compared with adults' spending power, it adds up to nearly $15 billion a year. And about $9 billion of that will actually be spent. Considering that a substantial portion is spent on food items—snack food and drinks—it is not surprising that so many new products are aimed at children.

In 1992, 46 percent of America's 13 million children aged 16 to 19 were employed. Almost three-quarters of these young people worked on a part-time basis in fast-food establishments, supermarkets, or other service-oriented industries, but paid wages account for only part of a teen's income. They also receive monetary gifts from other family members, allowances, and in some instances, such hard-to-track earnings as baby sitting compensation.

❙❙❙ SPENDING BY TEENS

In 1990, working teens living with two parents accounted for an average of 5 percent of before-tax family income. They earned an average of $2,611, or about $217 per month. And they certainly like to spend what they earn. Teen marketing expert Peter Zollo expected teenagers to spend $89 billion in 1994, of which $57 billion would come from their earnings and $32 billion would come from allowances and gifts. What do teens buy with all this money? The biggest category is athletic shoes, followed by clothing in general, blue jeans, groceries, and health-and-beauty aids.

A recent study by the New York-based Zandl Group looked at grocery spending by teens aged 13 to 18. In general, girls and boys have similar spending patterns, although girls spend somewhat more ($89 per month) than boys ($77 per month). Some 20 percent of girls and 18 percent of boys spend between $1 and $20 in the supermarket on a monthly basis. Almost 40 percent of teenaged girls spend between $21 and $50 per month in the supermarket. About 33 percent of teenaged boys spend this amount. Only 8 percent of girls and 10 percent of boys spend between $51 and $75 per month in the supermarket, and only 10 percent of girls and 11 percent of boys spend between $76 and $100. But about one-quarter of girls and an equal share of boys spend more than $100 in monthly supermarket purchases.

To most teenagers, a family outing to the supermarket is the thing nightmares are made of. Having to help mom with the weekly shopping is just plain boring. And it's not cool to have to tag along with younger siblings. But it's one of the ways to make sure that the latest rage in food makes it home. How else to persuade mom to buy the hottest cereal or the coolest soft drink?

Even if the grocery store is not as much fun as the mall, there are things to do, and more importantly, people to meet. And teens can use their money to buy the things they want—makeup, snack food, or magazines. One-third of teenaged girls visit the supermarket once a week, compared with one-quarter of teenaged boys, according to the New York-based Zandl Group. Thirty-one percent of teenaged girls and 27 percent of teenaged boys frequent the supermarket two or three times a month. Only 18 percent of girls and 19 percent of boys go once a month.

Teenaged boys are only slightly more likely than teenaged girls to be involved in family shopping while at the supermarket. While almost 30 percent of girls participate in the major shopping, 32 percent of boys do. But girls are more likely to go to the supermarket to pick up a few essentials—65 percent of girls versus only 41 percent of boys. Other reasons teens go to the supermarket include shopping for a special event or family meal, or stopping in to buy candy, magazines, or snacks.

A 1993 readers' poll conducted by *Seventeen* magazine looked at the shopping habits and spending patterns of its young women readers between the ages of 13 and 21. These shoppers go to the supermarket for themselves about as frequently as they go on shopping trips for the family. About one-quarter of them are doing the regular family shopping, as opposed to dashing to the store to pick up a few essentials.

The main reason teenaged girls like to go to the supermarket is to have the opportunity of picking out the products they want to have at home, according to the Zandl Group survey. While 31 percent identified this as the aspect of supermarketing they liked the best, 10 percent said that they welcomed the opportunity to see new products. A further 6 percent said that they liked buying food and having it at home.

The chance to buy food and have it available in the home was the main attraction of supermarket shopping to teenaged boys, with almost one-quarter citing it as the best-liked aspect of grocery shopping. Some 15 percent of boys also liked to pick the products they wanted at home, and 10 percent welcomed the chance to see new products. Unlike young adults, for whom supermarket shopping can be seen as an opportunity to meet people of the opposite sex, only 4 percent of teenaged boys and 2 percent of teenaged girls felt that supermarkets are a good place to pursue this opportunity.

The universal complaint of supermarket shoppers—long check-out lines—is also the main downer for teenagers. Fully 42 percent of teenaged girls and 37 percent of teenaged boys like this aspect of super-market shopping the least. The other things they don't like include having to spend too much time in the supermarket (19 percent of both sexes) and having to spend money (11 percent of girls and 12 percent of boys). They also complain about supermarket crowds (5 percent of girls and 7 percent of boys). But girls have a greater variety of com-plaints—having to push the cart, having too many choices, being tempted to buy things, having to deal with mean people, and just being bored by the whole thing.

The main attraction of the supermarket to teenaged girls has nothing to do with food. Almost one-quarter favor the health-and-beauty aids aisle, especially the make-up offerings. Equally attractive to girls is the produce department. Magazines are favored by 10 percent of teenaged girls, and 8 percent choose snack foods as their favorite area. Some 18 percent of boys prefer snack-food aisles, while 12 percent like the produce department. Ten percent of boys also favor the magazine section. Other departments favored by teens attest to their distinctive eating habits. They frequent the frozen food department, the candy and cereal aisles, and the bakery. While a small percentage of girls cited the salad bar and bulk-food sections as favorites, boys did not include these on their list. Some 3 percent of boys chose the seafood department, a selection not chosen by any teenage girls.

Girls are much more adamant about the department they don't like. One in four said that the meat department was their least favorite section, while 13 percent cited the frozen food aisles and 11 percent listed the cleaning products area as the worst part of the store. More boys dislike the produce department than like it. Fully 16 percent cited it as their least favorite part of the store. They also dislike the cleaning-supply aisle, the frozen-food area, the meat department, the front end, and not surprisingly, the feminine-hygiene aisle.

❙❚❙ KIDS IN THE KITCHEN

In the 1950s, when people talked about children learning to cook, the image that sprang to mind was that of a young baker making her first batch of sugar cookies or home-made fudge, accompanied by her stay-at-home mom. Mother and daughter wore matching aprons and big brother stood by, hungrily eyeing the freshly baked treats.

Times have changed. Kids in the kitchen of the 1990s are making their own meals and snacks. Boys and girls are familiar with the micro-wave, and more often than not, mom is still at work while they are whipping up pizzas, sandwiches, or cupcakes.

Boys are more likely than girls to use the microwave. Almost 26 percent of boys and about 18 percent of girls between the ages of 8 and 17 are microwave users, according to Good Housekeeping Institute's 1989 report on "Convenience Food and the Microwave." While younger girls (between the ages of 8 and 12) are slightly more likely to use this appliance than girls aged 13 to 17, older boys use the microwave slightly more than their younger counterparts.

Moms are more likely to allow their young children to use micro-wave ovens than conventional ovens. Some 38 percent of mothers sur-veyed by the American Frozen Food Institute (AFFI) in 1990 allowed their children between the ages of 5 and 8 to use a microwave independently. Only 6 percent allow children of the same age to use a conventional oven by themselves. Forty-eight percent of mothers allow their 9- to 12-year-olds to use the microwave oven alone.

Pre-teens are spending more time preparing food than ever before. Sixty-two percent of children under the age of 13 prepare one or more meals themselves each week, according to the AFFI survey. Twenty percent prepare at least four meals a week by themselves.

When kids are in the kitchen, their paths often go directly from freezer to microwave. Frozen pizza is their favorite frozen epicurean delight, chosen by 56 percent of kids. But other favorites attract a large share of youngsters, including frozen snacks (48 percent), frozen breads and breakfast foods (39 percent), and frozen entrees (21 percent).

Mothers quite happily let their kids have their own way with the microwave. Almost all mothers in the AFFI survey agreed that convenience was an important aspect of frozen food. More than three-quarters cited quick preparation as an asset. Other reasons for encouraging their young ones to use freezer-to-microwave foods included safety of preparation (51 percent), portion control (41 percent), and the nutritional balance of frozen food products (36 percent).

❙❚❚ A HEALTHY SNACK EVERY DAY

The emphasis placed on healthy eating is not restricted to adults. Children and teenagers are also being educated in school and on television about wise food choices. But even though thousands of educators teach children about the food pyramid and nutrition, the kids themselves are not making the grade when it comes to their real eating habits.

A 1988-9 survey by Harris/Scholastic Research commissioned by the Kellogg Company polled more than 5,000 children in grades 3 through 12 nationwide. While 43 percent of elementary-school children reported that they ate the right kinds of foods frequently, only 29 percent of senior high-schoolers did. One-third of latchkey kids could boast that they were frequent healthy eaters, compared with almost 40 percent of kids who came home to a parent or other guardian after school.

Children in grades 3 to 5 are more likely to say they eat healthy foods on a regular basis than their older friends in grades 6 to 12. Fully 60 percent of younger kids drink milk every day, and half say that they also eat fruit or drink fruit juices every day. Half of older kids drink milk every day, less than one-third drink fruit juice on a daily basis, and one in eight eats apples or bananas daily. Almost 40 percent of younger kids eat vegetables every day, while only 11 percent of older kids follow suit. And 26 percent of younger kids eat bread or toast daily, compared with 17 percent of older kids.

Younger kids eat cold cereals more often than older kids—both the unsweetened and the sweetened varieties. Children in grades 3 to 5 eat corn flakes, raisin bran, or other less-sweetened cereals about three times a week, compared with two times a week for the older children. The figures are the same for highly sweetened cereals such as Froot Loops, Cap'n Crunch, and Lucky Charms.

But both younger and older children eat a large variety of foods that are high in sugar, fat, and calories. Half of the children in grades 3 to 5 report that they drink soft drinks or other artificially sweetened beverages on a daily basis, as do an equal number of older kids. And 43 percent of kids of all ages say they eat cupcakes, cookies, candies, or Popsicles every day.

Although children are educated to identify foods that are nutritionally beneficial, they do not let that fact stand in the way of their food preferences. While only 6 percent of children think that soft drinks and other sweetened beverages are nutritionally "very good," 69 percent said that they liked those foods "very much." And while 58 percent acknowledged the health benefits of cooked broccoli or carrots, only 25 percent claimed to like them.

About one-third of children say they learn the most about good nutrition from their family, and 29 percent learn about food in school. But the lessons they learn may not always be reinforced by practice. Although family members play a role in food education, 53 percent of the children surveyed felt that they had more influence over what they ate than their parents or siblings did.

Setting a good example may be the best way to ensure that children eat properly. But only 38 percent of the children surveyed felt that their other family members frequently ate well. The majority (48 percent) felt that their family members ate well only sometimes.

In a 1990 AFFI survey, 54 percent of mothers said getting their kids to eat well-balanced meals was their biggest challenge when feeding them. Only 18 percent felt that their children ate too much junk food, 16 percent worried that their children consumed foods too high in fat and cholesterol, and just 10 percent were worried about their children eating too much sugar.

To help children learn about nutrition, many parents take them to the grocery store, according to AFFI. They let their kids have a say in some of the product choices, but only after limiting those choices to two or three nutritious options. Parents are also trying to set a better example in their own eating habits—they are reading food labels to ensure that they are buying nutritious foods—and they are trying to spend more quality kitchen time with their children.

Supermarketers are helping as well. A healthy-eating program called "Strive for Five" encourages the consumption of fresh fruits and vegetables with point-of-purchase material, sampling, promos, and incentives. Supermarketers also open their stores to class field trips so teachers can stress nutrition right in the store. At the same time, many stores are offering tours to school children so that they can see the way in which a supermarket functions.

▌▐ ▌ "WE WANT CHIPS"

Barney can shout his nutritious message until he turns from purple to blue, but kids are still big junk food junkies. While it is true that chips, popcorn, and pretzels are top salty snack choices, kids also eat sweet snacks like candy and cookies more than other groups. But with a little parental encouragement, they also eat a lot of fruit snacks.

The snacking patterns of children, especially youngsters aged 6 and younger, are more likely to be controlled by parents and doctors than by the children themselves. Most pediatricians advise against letting very young children eat snack nuts, since foods such as peanuts and cashews can pose a choking hazard. That helps explain why only 1 percent of heavy snack nut eaters are under age 6 and only about 6 percent are aged 6 to 12. Only 3 percent of heavy eaters of party mix, a snack that includes a percentage of nuts, are under 6, according to a 1992 survey by the Alexandria, Virginia-based Snack Food Association.

Kids account for a greater percentage of heavy snackers in other categories. Slightly more than 30 percent of heavy potato chip eaters are children aged 12 and younger, as are 38 percent of heavy tortilla chip eaters. Kids also make up the largest share of heavy eaters of extruded snacks like cheese puffs and cheese twists. Almost half of the heavy eaters of these types of snacks are aged 12 and younger.

Pretzels are often given by parents to their tiny teethers. And they are favored for older children because they are more or less fat free. Almost 40 percent of heavy pretzel eaters are aged 12 and younger, even though they account for only 19 percent of the total population. Children in this age group are also 25 percent of heavy corn chip consumers, and 38 percent of both heavy ready-to-eat popcorn eaters and heavy consumers of tortilla chips.

Teenagers do not consume savory snack foods as enthusiastically as children. They prefer more substantial snack foods like pizzas, subs, or fries. Among salty snacks, teens favor tortilla chips. Almost 11 percent of heavy tortilla chip eaters are aged 13 to 17, even though this group makes up 7 percent of the total population. They are also 11 percent of heavy consumers of ready-to-eat popcorn.

When teens go shopping, their favorite products are snack foods. This class of products was purchased by 95 percent of young regular female shoppers within the past two weeks, according to a 1993 *Seventeen* magazine readers' survey. Compare this with their likelihood of buying bread (72 percent), dairy items (73 percent), fresh meat and poultry (62 percent), or frozen foods (62 percent). Within the snack food category, salty snacks are slightly more popular than sweet snacks. Teenage girls also purchase carbonated soft drinks, milk, and juice, as well as cereals, chocolate, lunch meat, and canned soup.

The evolution of ready-to-eat cereal from breakfast fare to snack food illustrates the way in which children's and teenagers' snack habits have affected the food industry. Parents have for years given breakfast cereals to their toddlers as a healthy snack food—the small round or o-shaped oat or corn products are easy to chew, even for little tykes with one or two teeth, and they are nutritious. Accustomed to snacking on cereal, many kids will reach for a handful of oat squares or other crunchy cereal as an afternoon snack, and teens can be found eating cereal right out of the box at many points throughout the day. Cereal manufacturers, eager to expand their audience, have now begun to market cereal as snack food, thereby reaching two segments with the same product.

SECTION 2

ethnicity, regionality,
and locality

CHAPTER 6

Minority Markets
and Supermarkets

"AS AMERICAN as apple pie" is a cliché in need of an image make-over. America is no longer just pie. It is also bunellos, won tons, fritters, and papadums. And it is no longer just apples. Try mangoes, star fruit, lingonberries, or lichees. The increasing voice of ethnic and racial minorities, and the way in which they influence all things related to food, is creating great changes in the supermarket—in product mix, product display, and even in the products themselves.

Food manufacturers and supermarketers pay much more attention to minorities than ever before. In fact, all Americans, regardless of their race, religion, or ethnicity, are paying more attention to each other. Multiculturalism starts early—in day care centers, on television, in kids' coloring books, and in videos. Children are the heralds of the new multicultural America. They are encouraged to learn about their similarities and differences through games, books, toys, and even food.

Diversity starts with kids. Immigrants are usually young and mi-norities tend to have more children than whites; therefore, the younger population is more likely to be made up of people of different ethnic backgrounds than the population in general. While 80 percent of all Americans are white, according to the 1990 census, less than 75 percent of the population under age 10 is. Although 12 percent of all Americans are black, fully 15 percent of those under age 10 are. And even though Hispanics, an ethnic group that can be white, black, or any other racial category, account for 9 percent of the population in general, they are almost 13 percent of the population under age 10.

Although food is one of the most obvious factors that distinguishes people, it is also one of the most common ways for people to share their ethnic and racial identities. Marketers have found that many products destined for one segment of the population find their way into the shopping carts of others. But this was not always the case. During the 1950s, the most exotic cuisine a housewife or bachelor could prepare was classic French fare. Other tastes that occasionally made the transformation from restaurants to home kitchens were Italian and Chinese, in the guise of Americanized pastas and chop suey. Only the

The Minority Markets

The percent of the population that is white increases with age.

(total population by age, in thousands, and percent of total population by race and age, 1993)

age	total	white	black	other	Hispanic
total	257,927	83.2%	12.4%	4.3%	9.7%
less than 5	19,917	78.9	16.0	5.1	14.7
5 to 9	18,578	79.8	15.2	5.0	13.0
10 to 14	18,329	79.6	15.4	5.0	12.3
15 to 19	17,251	79.5	15.5	5.0	12.2
20 to 24	19,201	80.8	14.2	5.1	12.2
25 to 34	42,822	82.2	13.0	4.8	11.3
35 to 44	40,371	83.7	11.8	4.5	8.7
45 to 54	27,736	85.8	10.3	3.9	7.3
55 to 64	21,128	86.9	9.8	3.3	6.2
65 to 74	18,650	89.1	8.5	2.4	4.6
75 to 84	10,628	90.6	7.6	1.8	3.7
85 and older	3,315	91.1	7.4	1.5	3.6

Note: Hispanics may be of any race   Source: Bureau of the Census

most daring of amateur chefs ventured beyond these regulars to pre-pare such radical recipes as Polynesian pork or Spanish paella.

In 1990, salsa has become as ubiquitous as ketchup, and pizza and spaghetti are so mainstream, they're old hat. Kosher-certified labels appear on everything from colas to hot dogs. And just about every self-respecting fast-food place offers a range of multicultural dishes from tacos to bagels to croissants.

Today, there are two distinct topics to consider when looking at food and minorities. First, there is the question of marketing to minor-ity groups themselves. African Americans, Hispanics, Asians, and other minorities have their own distinct food cultures, tastes, and traditions. They also have a different set of economic and social parameters that set them apart from the mainstream when it comes to eating, cooking, and shopping. But minorities are not the only people interested in regional and ethnic cuisines. As more ethnic foods go mainstream, people of all ethnicities are crossing boundaries to try the latest foods.

Some manufacturers have begun to adapt ethnic recipes to suit non-ethnic tastes, while others are pushing cross-ethnic hybrids like Mexican pizza and Chinese pasta. And some products originally aimed at specific minorities have been "discovered" by shoppers who were looking for something different. Gerber found that its line of "Tropicals"—juices, dinners, cereals, and desserts in flavors like passion fruit, mango, and papaya—sold well not only to Hispanics, for whom the product was originally designed, but to other babies' parents as well.

Ethnic marketing has taken on new dimensions as different groups move from urban ethnic enclaves to more mixed suburbs and rural areas. Marketers who have never before seen any great ethnic diversity among their shoppers are now witnessing a broader variety of shoppers with different needs. Reaching these consumers requires a crash course in diversity. The results can be well worth the effort—as everyone, not just the minority shopper, begins to experiment with new products, new tastes, and new cooking ideas.

||| AFRICAN-AMERICAN CUSTOMERS

African Americans are the nation's largest minority, making up about 12 percent of the population. Estimates put their spending power some-

Blacks to 2000

During the 1990s, the total population of blacks in the U.S. will increase by 16 percent—to 35 million. Those aged 45 to 54 will increase 53 percent.

(black population by age, in thousands, 1990 and 2000, and percent change 1990-2000)

age	1990	2000	% change 1990-2000
total	30,483	35,469	16.4%
less than 5	2,939	3,214	9.4
5 to 9	2,711	3,302	21.8
10 to 14	2,629	3,141	19.5
15 to 19	2,714	3,057	12.6
20 to 24	2,655	2,668	0.5
25 to 34	5,498	5,235	-4.8
35 to 44	4,241	5,610	32.3
45 to 54	2,591	3,954	52.6
55 t 64	2,013	2,370	17.7
65 to 74	1,498	1,686	12.6
75 to 84	772	907	17.5
85 and older	223	326	46.2

Source: Bureau of the Census

where between $226 billion and $270 billion a year. About $36 billion is spent on food, 70 percent of which is spent on food at home, according to the 1992 Consumer Expenditure Survey.

African Americans in general are not as affluent as whites, but to stereotype them as poor would be a gross exaggeration. Thirty-nine percent of black households earned $25,000 or more in 1992. The number of black managers, teachers, doctors, and other professionals is rising. The median income of all black households in 1992 was almost $19,000. For households in their peak earning years (aged 45 to 54), the median income was $28,000.

The African American population is significantly younger than the white population in this country. In 1990, blacks had a median age of 28, compared with 35 for non-Hispanic whites. While the the median for blacks will reach 32 in 2050, the median for non-Hispanic whites is expected to rise to 45.

Not only is the African-American family usually younger, it is more often headed by a female householder than white households are. In fact, by 1994, more black families were headed by unmarried women than by married couples.

Black households are also more likely to be urban than other households. Just over 65 percent of blacks live in the 50 largest metropolitan areas of this country, compared with only 54 percent of whites. The largest black populations are concentrated in the metropolitan areas of New York, Chicago, Los Angeles, Philadelphia, and Washington, D.C. There are also sizable black populations in Detroit, Atlanta, Houston, Baltimore, and Miami.

African Americans make up more than 35 percent of the population of Mississippi. They account for more than a quarter of the population of Alabama, Georgia, South Carolina, and Louisiana, and between 15 and 25 percent of the population of New York, North Carolina, Virginia, Tennessee, Maryland, Arkansas, and Delaware. More than 65 percent of the population of the District of Columbia is black.

The black population is increasing in states in which they have traditionally been greatly underrepresented. In all regions except the

The Income Split

Across most age groups, median household income is highest for white householders and lowest for blacks.

(median household income, by race, Hispanic origin, and age of householder, 1992)

age	All races	white	black	Hispanic
all households	$30,786	$32,368	$18,660	$22,848
Less than 25	17,777	19,653	8,705	14,840
25 to 34	31,434	33,570	17,894	22,658
35 to 44	40,090	42,182	24,928	27,094
45 to 54	44,540	46,600	28,342	28,222
55 to 64	34,062	35,883	19,118	23,285
65 to 74	20,395	21,356	12,334	14,841
75 and older	13,622	14,111	7,931	10,986

Note: Hispanic can be of any race.

Source: Bureau of the Census

Living Lactose-Free

Milk and cookies, ice cream, Fettucini Alfredo, cheeseburgers, capuccino, and other milk products are a part of every American's diet. Right? Make that almost every American. The Northern European diet, rich in dairy products, is not for people of certain ethnic backgrounds who lack the ability to digest dairy products comfortably.

There are two conditions associated with milk sensitivity: common lactose intolerance and rarer allergic reactions to milk protein. People who are lactose intolerant lack the enzyme lactase—essential for the digestion of lactose or milk sugar. Without lactase, the lactose from milk products enters the small intestine undigested, causing intestinal pain, gas, bloating, and diarrhea. Attacks usually occur within 30 minutes of consuming a dairy product and are sometimes quite severe.

Milk protein allergy can manifest itself as an ear-nose-throat problem, a skin problem, or almost any medically undiagnosable discomfort from headaches to hyperactivity. Children with chronic ear infections may be sensitive to milk. And a 1992 study suggested that juvenile diabetes may be triggered by an infant's immune system response to the protein in cow's milk. Some experts have suggested eliminating milk altogether. "Milk is a perfect food for calves and is well-tolerated by some Caucasians, but for others it's a problem. I don't recommend milk for anyone," proclaimed Dr. Neal D. Barnard, Director of the Physicians Committee for Responsible Medicine (Washington, D.C.) in a 1993 press conference.

About 70 percent of the world's population, including 50 million Americans, may be lactose intolerant. And because most people suffer from a gradual decline in the production of lactase after the age of two, the numbers are sure to increase as the population ages. People from certain ethnic backgrounds are especially vulnerable. By their teens people of Asian ancestry, Native Americans, African Americans, Arab Americans, Jews, and people of Mediterranean stock exhibit increased symptoms of lactose intolerance. By the time they reach adulthood, half to three-quarters are lactose intolerant. About 70 percent of African

Americans and 85 percent of Asian Americans suffer from lactose intolerance. Lactase deficiency occurs in approximately 5 to 20 percent of Caucasian young adults.

Intolerance rates are similar for ethnic groups who live in different parts of the world. Jews living in the United States have a similar prevalence to those living in Israel. American blacks have a prevalence comparable to that of African blacks. Since some ethnic groups are more predisposed to it than others, lactose intolerance is considered hereditary.

So far, scientific research has not come up with a way of restoring lactase levels. The best way to treat the condition may be for each individual to figure out his or her tolerance level—which can vary widely. Most people can digest at least some milk products. They have few problems with aged cheeses, such as cheddar and Swiss, which are very low in lactose. Some can digest cultured milk products like yogurt, and others can tolerate milk if they drink it in very small portions throughout the day. Other lactose-intolerant individuals solve the problem by cutting out all dairy products, including products made with lactose, whey, or milk solids. But doing so may cause as many problems as it solves.

Milk and milk products are excellent sources of many nutrients, including calcium, protein, vitamin A, vitamin D, and riboflavin. Although most of these nutrients can be found in other sources, milk and milk products are among the best. Recent research concerning calcium intake suggests that even recommended daily allowances set forth by the government may not be adequate. Lactose intolerant people who choose simply to stop eating dairy products may get less than half of the recommended dietary allowance of calcium. Calcium deficiencies may play an important role in the development of bone-related disorders such as osteoporosis. While there are other ways of getting calcium into the diet, most Americans rely on milk.

continued...

Several commercial preparations can be added to milk to combat lactose intolerance. Lactaid, a Johnson & Johnson product, has practically cornered the market, according to scanner data from Information Resources, Incorporated. Other major products include Eastman Kodak's Dairy Ease and Thompson Medical's Lactogest. Companies are also marketing lactose-reduced and lactose-free dairy products, including milks and cheeses. Both Dairy Ease and Lactaid milks are available in whole, low-fat, and fat-free varieties. Lactaid makes chocolate and calcium-enriched versions. For those who want creamy desserts like ice cream or frozen yogurt, there is dairy-free Blis, a frozen dessert alternative to ice cream. The product is also fat free, lactose free, cholesterol free, sucrose free, preservative free, and free of artificial sweeteners.

In order to ensure that Americans get their calcium, manufacturers put extra calcium into other products. Calcium-fortified orange juice was introduced a number of years ago, and in 1994, Continental Baking Company of St. Louis, Missouri, introduced three varieties of its famous Wonder Bread with added calcium.

But other experts think that the recent publicity about lactose intolerance is hype. "From my perspective, lactose intolerance has been a fad for 30 years now," Dr. Douglas McGill of Mayo Medical School in Rochester, Minnesota told Time magazine in 1993. "There is nothing new except that business is after it." And after it in a big way. The lactose-intolerance industry has gone from a marginal existence several years ago to $117 million in sales in 1992, according to Information Resources, Inc. And the products are not cheap. Lactose-reduced milk, for instance, costs up to twice as much as ordinary milk.

But even the detractors concede that the lactose-intolerance industry is not completely without foundation. The growing populations of blacks and Asians are demanding more lactose-free products. And aging baby boomers will further fuel demand for the dairy products they loved before they developed lactose intolerance.

Midwest, the black population increased more than 10 percent between 1980 and 1990. In the West, the black population increased by 25 percent during that decade. The biggest increases were in New Hampshire (80 percent), Minnesota (78 percent), and Vermont (72 percent). Other states with large increases were Alaska (65 percent) and Maine (64 percent).

I I ■ AFRICAN-AMERICAN FOOD

Even though the typical African-American consumer unit* is large (2.8 persons per household versus 2.5 for households in general), they spend less on food than others. The average annual expenditure for food at home by blacks is $2,200, but $2,640 for all Americans, according to the 1992 Consumer Expenditure Survey.

African Americans spend less on milk and dairy products than other groups in part because of their high incidence of lactose intolerance. But they spend more on certain products than whites and others do. Although African Americans spend less overall on cereals and cereal products than others, they spend more on rice ($17 per year versus $12) and flour ($10 versus $7). They are heavier meat consumers than most. They spend $736 per year on meats, poultry, fish and eggs, compared with $681 for whites and others. The biggest difference in meat spending is in the pork category. African Americans spend $188 annually on pork products, compared with $152 for whites and others. The only pork category in which blacks spend less than whites and others is ham ($37 per year by blacks versus $43 per year by whites and others).

Whether it's fresh or frozen, whole or pieces, African Americans spend more on poultry than whites and others ($133 annually versus $122). And African Americans also spend more on all classes of fish and seafood, except canned fish and seafood. African Americans spend 74 percent more on fresh and frozen fin fish—$59 in 1992, compared with $34 for whites and others.

Spending patterns in most other categories are similar, but African Americans spend about three-quarters as much as whites on peanut

---

The Bureau of Labor Statistics' consumer units are not exactly comparable to households as defined by the Bureau of the Census.

butter ($9 annually, compared with $12). And they spend half as much as whites and others on canned and packaged soups ($13, compared with $26). They spend more than others on noncarbonated fruit-flavored drinks ($25 versus $19), sugar ($23 versus $17), and eggs ($29 versus $28).

Blacks and whites use different products; they also use the same products in different ways, according to Eugene Morris, president of Chicago-based E Morris, Ltd. Morris suggests that many eating habits are rooted in past traditions. For example, Morris points out that blacks are less likely than whites to eat rare meat, a habit he traces back to the last century, when enslaved and poor blacks were unable to obtain prime cuts of meat. He also suggests that the heavier consumption of meats classified as "other" —chitterlings, pigs' feet, and organ meat— by blacks is a throwback to those same days, when slaves ate only less than the best meat products.

Morris points out that most blacks want something sweet with their meals. For that reason, they are heavier than average consumers of sugar, which they add to unsweetened fruit juice mixes, coffee, or tea. They also consume large quantities of presweetened beverages.

The Racial Market Basket

Black households spend only half as much as white/other households on coffee, but they spend more on poultry.

(average household expenditures for selected grocery products, by race, 1992)

product	all consumers	white/other	black
Fresh fruit	$127.39	$129.90	$107.73
Milk and cream	133.81	139.95	85.65
Fresh vegetables	126.58	129.92	100.41
Poultry	123.10	121.80	133.28
Ground beef	86.66	86.75	85.94
Bread	76.28	77.36	67.81
Potato chips/nuts/snacks	75.64	79.02	49.16
Nonprescription drugs	74.51	77.53	50.82
Toilet paper/tissues	56.62	57.89	46.66
Coffee	38.95	41.26	20.86

Source: Bureau of Labor Statistics, 1992 Consumer Expenditure Survey

I I ■ AFRICAN-AMERICAN MARKETS

Long recognized as being brand loyal, the African-American shopper is a steadfast ally for large food manufacturers who have recently been losing market share to generics and store brands. "Even those (African Americans) with limited funds will buy brand names—names they can trust," says Sandra Miller Jones, chairperson of Segmented Marketing Services, Inc. (SMSi). Although black brand loyalty is strong, they have been buying more generics, she adds. That is why Quaker Oats, Coca-Cola, Pillsbury, and other large marketers have been targeting African-American shoppers more energetically than ever.

Marketers are taking notice of African Americans, their traditions, and their needs. "African Americans *aren't* little brown white people," says Lafayette Jones, president and CEO of SMSi. Marketers should "look at the market not in terms of black and white, but in terms of true ethnicity. We use 'European American' and 'African American' because these terms really describe what we're talking about, without the social and political implications of race... Every different culture has its own food, music, religious practices. They're diverse in competition, flavorings, attitudes, and expressions," says Jones.

Supermarketers trying to reach this segment require sensitivity to and knowledge about African-American cultural and social traditions, not to mention their eating and shopping habits. The Pillsbury Company features peach cobbler, not cherry pie, when targeting its premade pie crusts to black audiences. It also replaced the brawny white lumberjacks in Pillsbury's advertisements for Hungry Jack biscuits. And African-American role models are the spokespeople for Coca-Cola, Wheaties, and a host of other products.

Even within categories, certain products attract greater African-American loyalty than others. Even though they are only about 21 percent of the population, blacks and Hispanics account for 40 percent of consumers of lemon-lime soda and 50 percent of fruit flavored (grape or orange) soda. After Coca-Cola began advertising Fanta orange soda on black-adult contemporary radio stations, the beverage experienced an impressive 2.1 percent increase in market share.

Marketing to the African-American market requires knowing how to reach them. As urban residents, they are often ignored by direct mail marketers, including food manufacturers and retailers, who use direct mail for the distribution of coupons and samples. Many marketers only target single-family units, thus ignoring large numbers of urban minority apartment dwellers.

African Americans are not great coupon users for a number of reasons. Many of them do not subscribe to the Sunday papers in which the majority of coupons are distributed. Urban blacks often shop at inner-city stores which do not accept coupons on a regular basis. In fact, "There is a certain pride in *not* using them," according to SMSi's Lafayette Jones. "Couponing is just not an effective tool in reaching the African-American market." Jones' observation is backed up by a 1994 survey conducted by Market Segment Research, Incorporated of Coral Gables, Florida. Only 43 percent of African Americans reported using coupons in the past 30 days, compared with 66 percent of whites.

On the other hand, African Americans are very receptive to sampling—either in-store or by some direct marketing plan. Mature shoppers especially like trying before buying. African Americans also enjoy the attention they receive from large corporations who target them for sampling. SMSi targets playing fields by offering "point of sweat" sampling of products where local or regional baseball, basketball, or football teams practice. Other venues for advertising products include music festivals, night clubs, and sporting event venues.

SMSi also successfully reaches African Americans through its "Church Family Network"—a network of 7,000 African-American and Hispanic churches. African Americans are more likely to go to church on a regular basis than whites, and their involvement in their regular place of worship is often strong. "The role of the church in black family and consumer life is very big," says Sandra Miller Jones of SMSi. "The black church is more of a secular, economic, and political center than general churches are," she says.

The churches receive gift bags emblazoned with African-American or Hispanic icons and the logo "A Gift from Companies Who Care." The products come from the country's top marketers, who use this network to reach previously unreachable—but potentially hugely profitable—

market segments. Having felt shunned or ignored by large marketers in the past, the recipients are pleased to be on the receiving end of the deal. An average of 80 percent of recipients try the samples, and half of those convert to the products, according to Lafayette Jones. Supermarketers can also reach their African-American constituency with in-store sampling. Both products consumed on the premises and carried-out items create opportunities for African-American brand loyalty.

Another way in which marketers and manufacturers can reach African Americans is through community involvement. "The relationship with the customer does not end at the cash register," says Ken Smikle, president of the African-American Marketing and Media Association. African-American consumers look for relevant advertising messages, but they are also looking for community involvement and minority hiring. Because African Americans want to spend their money in stores that give something back to the community, supermarkets with strong community-based programs and recognized efforts to hire minority workers garner loyalty from this important market segment.

❙❙❙ AFRICAN-AMERICAN NUTRITION

The typical African American's diet is high in fat, according to a 1994 study of adults who shop regularly for their households, conducted by *Prevention* magazine and the Food Marketing Institute (FMI). On average, 43 percent of blacks eat high fat meat and eggs 7 to 14 times a week. An additional 17 percent consume these fatty foods 15 or more times a week. On average, one-fourth of whites eat these foods once a day, and only 5 percent eat them 15 or more times per week.

Blacks are also more likely than whites to eat chicken with the skin on. Sixty-six percent did so at least once in the past week, compared with only 30 percent of whites. Slightly more than 80 percent of blacks eat eggs at least once a week, compared with 74 percent of whites. Both blacks and whites are equally heavy consumers of hamburger, sausage, or bacon. But African-American shoppers eat a wide variety of lean meats as well. They are more likely than whites to eat fish or seafood at least once a week (80 percent versus 75 percent).

Eating a diet that is high in fiber is an important factor in maintaining good health, but African Americans are less likely than whites to eat large quantities of fiber-rich foods. While three-fourths of whites eat high-fiber foods 15 or more times a week, only 61 percent of African Americans do. Half of African Americans eat fruit and vegetables 7 to 14 times a week, compared with 44 percent of whites. But whites are more likely to eat these items frequently. Forty-one percent of whites eat fruit and vegetables 15 or more times a week, compared with 31 percent of African Americans. African Americans are less likely to eat pasta, whole-grain bread, or brown rice frequently. Only 13 percent African Americans eat these types of foods at least 15 times a week, compared with 23 percent of whites.

African Americans eat considerably fewer dairy products than whites. This difference may in part result from the larger share of blacks who suffer from lactose intolerance. Fifteen percent of African Americans eat milk, cheese, or yogurt 15 to 21 times a week, compared with 28 percent of whites. While 12 percent of African Americans say they never eat dairy products, only 3 percent of whites say they eat none. African Americans are also less likely to use fats and oils at every meal. Eleven percent used these products between 15 and 21 times a week, compared with 20 percent of whites. Only 7 percent use them more frequently, compared with 13 percent of whites.

Consumer education is essential for teaching African Americans ways in which they can improve their diets. In the 1992 *Prevention* magazine/FMI survey, shoppers were asked the best way to reduce the risk of serious health problems. One in five African Americans suggested avoiding foods high in saturated fat, compared with one in three whites. And 17 percent of African Americans thought that avoiding foods with high cholesterol would be most beneficial to reduce disease, compared with 27 percent of whites.

On the other hand, African Americans have a higher prevalence of high blood pressure and hypertension and are more aware than whites of the importance of limiting salt and sodium (29 percent, compared with 14 percent of whites). They are not, however, as careful about their intake of sugar, even though blacks have a higher incidence of diabetes than whites. About 9 blacks per 1,000 under the age of 45 have this disease, compared with slightly more than 7 per 1000 whites, according to 1992 figures from the National Center for Health Statistics. Among people aged 65 and older, blacks have diabetes at twice the rate of whites—199 per 1,000, compared with 102 per 1,000.

Corporations such as Quaker Oats have responded to the needs of its black customers by advertisements that focus on the health benefits of its products. Whole-grain cereals are being targeted to African-American mothers concerned about their families' health. And the company is going further. In cooperation with its philanthropic arm, it is focusing on a program promoting nutrition and health among African Americans.

I ∎ HISPANIC-AMERICAN CUSTOMERS

The Bureau of the Census defines "Hispanic" as a person who identifies himself or herself as of Hispanic origin. Hispanics may be of any race. They may speak Spanish or be of Spanish-speaking ancestry. Hispanics can be light- or dark-skinned. They can be from Central or South America, or from Europe. They can speak English at home, or they can use Spanish exclusively.

There is no such thing as a single Hispanic market. Mexican Americans have different traditions than Guatemalan Americans. Cuban Americans may have different aspirations than Colombian Americans. Older Hispanics are different from younger ones. Suburban Hispanics are not the same as inner-city dwellers. And foreign-born Hispanics have different ideas about products and services than U.S.-born Hispanics. To understand this market, you must understand not only what Hispanics have in common with each other, but also how the various groups differ.

In 1990, there were 23 million Hispanics in the United States—about 9 percent of the total population. They are the second largest minority group, but the population is growing rapidly. By 2000, they will number 31 million, and by 2010, they will reach 41 million, edging out blacks as America's largest minority, according to Census Bureau projections.

The median income of Hispanic households remained more or less stable in the early 1990s, according to the Census Bureau. Young householders—those between the ages of 25 and 34—saw an increase of less than $1,000 in median income, from $21,700 to $22,700. The median income of Hispanic householders between the ages of 35 and 44 increased by only $400, from $26,600 to $27,000. And Hispanics in their peak earning years, aged 45 to 54, had incomes which remained stagnant, at about $28,200, in 1990 and 1992. Hispanic householders aged 55 to 64 actually saw a drop in their median income between 1990 and 1992, from $24,800 to $23,300.

The median income of Hispanic households is higher than that of black households in all age groups except those aged 45 to 54. But even in that peak-earning group, households with primary earners between the ages of 45 and 54, it is still below $30,000, according to 1992 figures from the Bureau of the Census.

Hispanics to 2000

Hispanic baby boomers will cause those aged 35 to 44 to grow 71 percent in the 1990s.

(Hispanic population by age, in thousands, 1990 and 2000, and percent change 1990-2000)

age	1990	2000	% change 1990-2000
total	22,354	31,166	39.4%
less than 5	2,467	3,293	33.5
5 to 9	2,178	3,232	48.4
10 to 14	1,989	2,846	43.1
15 to 19	2,084	2,624	25.9
20 to 24	2,320	2,489	7.3
25 to 34	4,382	5,145	17.4
35 to 44	2,909	4,830	66.0
45 to 54	1,686	3,046	80.7
55 t 64	1,183	1,734	46.6
65 to 74	715	1,137	59.0
75 to 84	339	586	72.9
85 and older	91	203	123.1

Note: Hispanics may be of any race.

Source: Bureau of the Census

The term "Hispanic" covers a wide array of people. While most Hispanics in the U.S. today are of Mexican, Puerto Rican, or Cuban ancestry, a growing number come from other Latin-American nations. "Because Hispanics of all kinds live together in small areas, each country of origin can form a visible and desirable target market," says Morton Winsberg of Florida State University in Tallahassee.

Understanding the specific Hispanic origins of shoppers is important to food marketers. Although the population is linked by a common language, the cultural and economic differences of each group can affect shopping patterns, food choice, and food spending. Marketers can also take advantage of the Hispanic diversity by acknowledging festivals, traditions, and foods specific to the cultures most highly represented in the store's customer base.

The largest group, Mexican Americans, account for 61 percent of Hispanics, or about 14 million people. Almost one-quarter of Hispanics of Mexican origin live in or around Los Angeles. The other top urbanized areas settled by Mexican Americans are Chicago, Houston, San Antonio, and San Diego. The fastest-growing sub-segment of the U.S. Hispanic population, Mexicans accounted for almost 9 percent of all legal immigrants to this country in 1990. But many Mexican-American families have lived in Texas and other parts of the Southwest since before these territories became part of the U.S.

The Mexican-American population is the youngest of the major Hispanic national groups, according to the 1990 census. Their median age is 24, compared with a median of nearly 33 years for Americans in general. Five percent of Mexicans aged 25 or older are college graduates, compared with 21 percent of all Hispanics and 41 percent of all Americans. Their median income in 1989 was $22,000, compared with $22,000 for all Hispanics and $30,000 for all Americans. One in four Mexican Americans lives below the poverty line, compared with 11 percent of all Americans.

About 12 percent of Hispanics, or 2.6 million Americans, are of Puerto Rican origin. All Puerto Ricans are of course citizens, because Puerto Rico is a territory of the United States. Forty-four percent of Puerto Ricans living in the "lower 48" reside in New York City. Other big centers for Puerto Rican communities are Chicago, Philadelphia,

Miami, and Los Angeles. Puerto Ricans are the second-youngest Hispanic population overall, with a median age of about 27. More Puerto Ricans than Mexicans have attended some college (10 percent), but as a group, they are more likely to live below the poverty line (38 percent). The median income for Puerto Ricans on the mainland is just $16,000.

Cuban Americans are 5 percent of all Hispanics, with about 1 million residents in the United States. They are the richest and oldest of the major Hispanic sub-segments, with a median age of 39 and a median 1989 income of nearly $26,000. Only 14 percent of Cuban Americans live below the poverty line, and 19 percent have had some post-secondary education. More than half of the Cuban-American population lives in Miami. Other sizable Cuban populations can be found in New York, Los Angeles, Tampa-St. Petersburg, and Fort Lauderdale.

About 22 percent of Hispanics are of other national origins. The median age of Central and South Americans is 27 years, and their median 1989 income was $24,000. Some 15 percent have attended college, but 22 percent live below the poverty level. Populations of El Salvadorans, Dominicans, Columbians, Gautemalans, Nicaraguans, Ecuadorans, Peruvians, Hondurans, and Panamanians have been growing during the past decade. More often than not, new immigrants will join already-settled family members and create growing concentrations of Hispanics in specific major metropolitan areas. But new Hispanic immigrants are less likely than previous generations to live in ethnic-specific neighborhoods, making them very difficult to target.

Half of the 565,000 people who have El Salvadoran roots have settled in the Los Angeles metro area. The rest are to be found in New York, Washington, D.C., San Francisco, and Houston. More than three-quarters of the 520,000 Hispanics whose origins lie in the Dominican Republic are living in New York City. But Dominicans have also settled in Miami, Boston, Lawrence, Massachusetts, and Providence, Rhode Island.

In 1990, there were 379,000 Americans of Colombian origin. The largest share (40 percent) can be found in New York City, but Miami, Los Angeles, Fort Lauderdale, and Houston have also attracted many Colombians. Guatemalan Americans (269,000) are concentrated in Los

Angeles, New York, Chicago, San Francisco, and Washington, D.C. About a third of the 203,000 people of Nicaraguan origin have settled in Miami. Others live in Los Angeles, San Francisco, New York, and Washington, D.C.

Sixty percent of the 191,000 Hispanics of Ecuadoran origin live in New York. Ecuadorans also have established sizable enclaves in Los Angeles, Chicago, Miami, and Washington, D.C. America's 175,000 Peruvians favor New York, Los Angeles, Miami, Washington, D.C., and San Francisco. One-quarter of America's 131,000 Hondurans live in New York. They have also settled in Los Angeles, Miami, New Orleans, and Houston. The 92,000 Panamanians prefer to live in New York, Miami, Los Angeles, Washington, D.C., and San Francisco.

While some urban areas are noted for specific Hispanic groups, recent census data show that these neighborhoods are not necessarily their exclusive residence. While Cubans in the Miami area flock to "Little Havana" to shop, socialize, and eat, almost 43 percent of Hispanics live in the suburbs of the largest metropolitan areas. Hispanics who have chosen suburban living tend to be more affluent than those who have remained in the city. But suburban Hispanics who live in heavy concentrations have lower incomes than those who live in suburbs with small shares of Hispanics.

Whether Hispanics live in suburbs or in inner cities, they still want to keep in contact with their Hispanic heritage. Many Hispanics view shopping as a social event, and as a way of keeping in contact with news of families and the "old country." It is not unusual for suburban Hispanics to drive to older, established shopping areas more closely associated with their own heritage. For that reason, it is important for local supermarketers to understand the make-up of their constituent populations, and to provide incentives for them to shop closer to home. Understanding the type of Hispanics that live in the neighborhood and targeting those subgroups with specific products or premiums may give them more reasons to shop locally.

|I■ HISPANIC FOODS

On average, Hispanic households spend more on most products than non-Hispanic households. But Hispanic households are considerably larger than those of non-Hispanics. The average size is 3.4 people, compared with 2.5 for non-Hispanics.

Hispanics spend more per capita on meat, poultry, fish, and eggs ($373) than non-Hispanics ($279), and on fresh vegatables ($72 versus $51). In all other general categories, they spend less. Detailed breakdowns are not available from the Consumer Expenditure Survey.

Hispanics are more likely than the general population to be heavy purchasers of regular (non-diet) carbonated soft drinks (72 percent versus 64 percent), diet carbonated soft drinks (30 percent versus 28 percent), butter (70 percent versus 58 percent), cooking oil (91 percent versus 79 percent), and dry pasta (53 percent versus 42 percent), according to the 1994 MSR *Ethnic Market Report.*

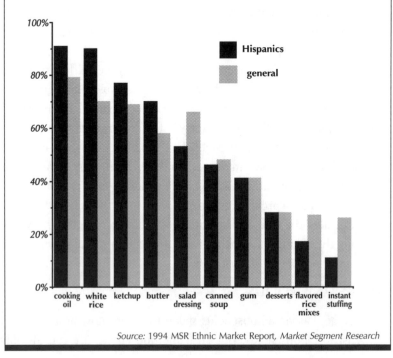

Hispanics' Love of Rice and Oil

Hispanics are more likely than the general shopping public to purchase white rice, butter, and cooking oil in a typical month.

(percent of selected items that the Hispanic and general market purchased in the past month, 1994)

Source: 1994 MSR Ethnic Market Report, *Market Segment Research*

Because milk is a big seller in the Hispanic market, there is some specialty marketing of this product. Leche Fresca, distributed by the Goya Company, is a whole milk product with a 3.8 percent fat content, compared with regular whole milk, which has a 3.25 percent fat content. "Many Hispanics have grown up in countries where this higher fat milk is the norm. They have grown accustomed to this rich flavor and prefer it over whole milk," says Marc Goldman, president of Farmland Dairies in Wallington, New Jersey. "And as the Hispanic population continues to grow, serving the needs of this market segment makes good business sense."

Birthplace affects certain shopping and eating patterns, according to the Market Development/Yankelovich Hispanic MONITOR 1992. Foreign-born Hispanics use fruits and vegetables from their home countries more regularly than Hispanics born in this country. Fully 85 percent of foreign-born Hispanics aged 16 and older use Latin-American fruit, and 78 percent use Latin-American vegetables on a regular

The Native Hispanic

Foreign-born Hispanics are more likely than U.S.-born Hispanics to use Latin fruits and vegetables.

(percent of selected foods used in the household regularly by foreign-born Hispanics and U.S.-born Hispanics aged 16 and older, 1992)

product	foreign-born Hispanics	U.S.-born Hispanics
Latin fruits	85%	61%
Latin vegetables	78	54
Hispanic-style cheese	75	48
Mayonnaise	66	72
Cold cuts	56	71
Gelatin dessert	44	36
Peanut butter	41	51
Canned vegetables	26	40
Cake mix	22	34
Frozen dinners	15	23

Source: Market Development/Yankelovich Hispanic MONITOR, 1992

basis at home. About 61 percent of U.S.-born Hispanics use these more exotic fruits, and 54 percent of them use the Latin-American vegetables. Hispanics born outside the U.S. are also more likely to use Hispanic-style cheese (75 percent) than those Hispanics born in the U.S. (48 percent).

On the other hand, foreign-born Hispanicsare less likely to use frozen vegetables (30 percent) than their U.S.-born compatriots (41 percent) and they are also less likely to use single-sliced cheese (64 percent versus 71 percent). Other foods that are used less regularly by foreign-born Hispanics include peanut butter (41 percent versus 51 percent), popcorn (47 percent versus 61 percent), and pretzels (26 percent versus 31 percent).

American-born Hispanics, those who have assimilated into U.S. culture, and those who primarily speak English at home, eat fewer Latin-American fruits, vegetables, and cheeses than others. Eighty-two percent of consumers from primarily Spanish-speaking households use Latin varieties of fruits on a regular basis, according to the 1992 Market Development/Yankelovich Hispanic MONITOR. Only 54 percent of those from primarily English-speaking households do. Eight in ten Spanish-speaking households use Latin-style vegetables, compared with about half of English-speaking households. And 77 percent use Hispanic-style cheese, compared with only 33 percent of primarily English-speaking households.

Hispanics are more likely to be heavy purchasers of over-the-counter (non-prescription) medications, according to the *1994 MSR Ethnic Market Report* from Market Segment Research, Incorporated of Coral Gables, Florida. Many Hispanics do not have health insurance and many also have limited incomes. Instead of seeking help from a medical professional for minor ailments, Hispanics will first try to cure themselves.

While 43 percent of the general population purchased analgesics (aspirin and ibuprofein) in the month before the survey, 58 percent of Hispanics did so. Thirty-seven percent of Hispanics purchased antacids, compared with 30 percent of the total population. Hispanics are also more likely to buy products such as cough syrup (41 percent versus 35 percent) and stomach remedies (40 percent versus 30 percent).

I I ■ SPEAKING TO HISPANICS

Along with the problem of trying to sub-segment the Hispanic population by country of origin, marketers must also come to grips with the
issue of language. Not all Hispanics speak English. Some speak only
Spanish, and some are bilingual. Marketers recognize three different
language segments: "Spanish-dominate Hispanics," who read, write,
and think in the language; "English-dominate Hispanics," who are second or third-generation Americans, proud of their Hispanic heritage,
but having only a limited or even non-existent command of the Spanish
language; and "Bilinguals," who make up the majority of the Hispanic
market.

Which language should marketers use? It depends on your customers, but some specialists maintain that bilingual signage and personnel are important even if the majority of consumers speak both
languages. "The use of Spanish in Hispanic sections of New York, New
Jersey, and Miami is considered a courtesy, a sign of respect. It is well
received," says Peter Costa, president of the Huntington, New York-
based Target Marketing company.

Using Spanish and English reaches more Hispanics than using
only English, even if a large majority of a store's customers are bilingual. "Hispanics have not integrated as quickly as earlier immigrant
groups. Because of their frequent contact with their homelands and
their local concentrations within the U.S., Hispanics cling to their language and culture," writes Ronald D. Michman, author of *Lifestyle
Market Segmentation*. Giving them an option to read about new products or to find out about a store's specials in both languages is the most
thorough way of reaching the lion's share of customers.

"One of the best media buys in a Mexican/Latino neighborhood is
its bilingual community newspaper. If your constituency is made up of
a number of Mexican/Latino subgroups, use advertising dollars wisely.
Spend some on Spanish only, some on English only, and some on bilingual circulars, point-of-purchase signage, and so on," says Jerome
Wilson Lloyd, editor of *MAGAzine,* the monthly publication of the Los
Angeles-based Mexican American Grocers Association.

Lloyd feels that in order for a supermarket to be successful in an

Hispanic community, the retailer must also use a degree of "micro-marketing." "Changing demographics can mean more than one thing. Your neighborhood may change to predominantly Mexican/Latino, but it goes beyond that. Is your constituency new immigrants; second, third, or fourth generation Mexican/Latino; young, single Mexican/Latinos; Mexican/Latino families with young children; middle-aged Mexican/Latinos whose children have left home, and so on?" Lloyd suggests identifying the type of customer by age and social situation to determine the product mix and the services a store should offer. "Lifestyles are always changing, and a good retailer can respond to these changes almost as quickly as they happen and he or she keeps an eye open for food purchasing patterns that occur among all demographic groups."

I I ∎ HISPANIC LOYALTY

Hispanics are less likely than Anglos to use coupons when shopping, according to MSR's *1994 Ethnic Market Report*. While 66 percent of Anglos used coupons within the 30 days prior to the survey, only 44 percent of Hispanics did. The kinds of coupons that appeal most to Hispanics are the "buy one, get one free" variety, and those giving cents off the purchase price of the product. Hispanics are not likely to take advantage of rebate-style coupons.

In order to attract more Hispanics, coupon issuers are beginning to use English and Spanish on the coupons. While 55 percent of coupons Hispanics used were in English only in 1994, 34 percent were bilingual. Eleven percent were issued in Spanish only.

Although Hispanics are not big coupon users, their brand loyalty is worth note. But brand loyalty has two sides. Brands that are familiar in Latin America often fare better among Hispanics in the U.S. than brands that are new to them. But Hispanics who have assimilated into American culture may prefer a brand that is better known in the U.S. A brand typically associated with the U.S. will be a big seller in areas where English or bilingualism predominates. But a brand that is heavily advertised in Latin America will fare well in communities where Spanish is the main language and where the majority of residents are foreign-born, according to Thomas Weyr, author of *Hispanic U.S.A.: Breaking the Melting Pot.*

But Kay Schultz Mount, executive vice president for NuStats, Incorporated of Austin, Texas, maintains that Hispanic brand loyalty is a myth. While many Hispanics are not aware of mainstream products in the U.S., they are aware of products that are well-known in their home countries. Still, if that brand is not available, Hispanics will look for brands that reflect their native values and culture.

Both experts are right. Hispanics who are new to America will seek out the familiar. Those who come from small villages in their homelands will not be aware of the multitude of American brands available. They will choose the brand they bought at home, in part because of loyalty to the brand, but also because they are familiar with that brand and know what to expect from it. Assimilated and acculturated Hispanics will move on to American brands as a way of identifying with their new culture and their new land.

The Market Development/Yankelovich Hispanic MONITOR 1992 backs up this assertion. Almost three-quarters of Hispanics agreed that they prefer to buy products made by well-established companies. And 71 percent find that it is very difficult to change brands once they have found one they like. Only 57 percent felt that store brands are better than well-known, nationally advertised brands, and only 52 percent felt that all brands are the same.

❚❚❚ HISPANIC MARKETS

Where Hispanics shop depends in part on whether they are foreign-born or U.S. born, and whether they are English-speaking, Spanish-speaking, or bilingual. The single most commonly used food outlet is the supermarket, which is used by 83 percent of Hispanics on a monthly basis. More U.S.-born Hispanics shop at supermarkets than foreign-born Hispanics (87 percent versus 81 percent), according to the Market Development/Yankelovich Hispanic MONITOR 1992. Eighty-eight percent of English speakers use the supermarket on a monthly basis, compared with 86 percent of bilingual Hispanics, and 80 percent of Spanish speakers.

Less than one-third of Hispanics shop for food in convenience stores on a monthly basis. Half of American-born Hispanics use convenience stores, compared with about one-fourth of foreign-born Hispanics. About one-fourth of Spanish speakers shop that format, compared with half of English speakers, according to the Market Development/ Yankelovich Hispanic MONITOR 1992.

Some 78 percent of Hispanics frequent a neighborhood food store. Eighty-one percent of foreign-born shoppers feel more comfortable in a neighborhood store, compared with 69 percent of U.S.-born Hispanic shoppers. And 79 percent of Spanish speakers frequent neighborhood stores for food, compared with 74 percent of English speakers and 73 percent of bilingual shoppers.

The biggest difference in shopping patterns can be seen at bodegas—local grocery stores in which the predominant language is Spanish and the atmosphere is distinctly Hispanic. Two-thirds of foreign-born Hispanics shop at bodegas once a month, compared with half of U.S.-born Hispanics. About two-thirds of primarily Spanish speakers shop in these outlets, compared with only 43 percent of primarily English-speaking Hispanics. About 57 percent of bilingual shoppers use this type of store once a month.

▍▮ HISPANIC GROCERIES

Hispanics are very family and community oriented. They seek to maintain their culture and heritage in a number of ways—through community events, music, the church—and grocery shopping. "Along with providing a nearby location for convenient purchases, the bodega (neighborhood grocery store) was found to serve the important role of maintaining Latin culture," concludes Carol J. Kaufman, assistant professor of marketing at Rutgers University and Sigfredo A. Hernandez, assistant professor of marketing at Rider College.

Bodegas in Hispanic inner-city communities (barrios) serve as social gathering centers as well as places to pick up food products. The average bodega purchase is only about $10, but most customers visit their neighborhood bodega every day, say Kaufman and Hernandez.

What do Hispanics get at bodegas? Gossip, news of home, ideas about where to find a job, buy a car, or rent an apartment, and food items such as rice, canned beans, and tropical produce. Bodegas are easy to get to. They are usually the only store within walking distance. They are comfortable, the conversation is in Spanish, the brands are familiar, and the whole atmosphere is an "oasis of Latin culture."

Bodegas do not always offer the same services provided by Anglo neighborhood stores. They are less likely to accept cents-off coupons, to cash checks, and to help customers with tax or other forms, according to Kaufman and Hernandez. However, they are more likely than Anglo retailers to accept food stamps, and extend credit to loyal customers.

But bodegas' main asset is Latino culture. The foods, smells, and sounds of home proliferate, say Kaufman and Hernandez. Hispanic shoppers, especially foreign-born shoppers, feel right at home. For that reason, the bodega will continue to flourish as an alternative outlet for Hispanic grocery shoppers.

Taking a leaf from the pages of bodega marketing, Tianguis, an Hispanic supermarket in Los Angeles, conducted studies of food shopping habits of Mexicans and Mexican Americans. They designed their store to reflect the needs of its Hispanic clientele. The store stresses the community aspect of shopping, especially family values and community. Hispanic brands and products are featured, employees are bilingual, and the qualities sought after by Hispanic shoppers—freshness, quality, and value—are emphasized.

Understanding the lure of the bodega is important for supermarketers who wish to reach the Hispanic population. Competition with the bodega may not be possible for the large food store. No supermarket can duplicate the feeling of a small, family-oriented, neighborhood bodega. And the bodega will continue to be a center of Latino culture as long as Hispanics maintain ties with their home countries and traditions—and as long as immigration from Latin America continues to bring large numbers of foreign-born Hispanics to this country.

But supermarketers can study the bodega and duplicate some of its features. At least some employees in a large food store should be bilingual if a store wants to attract Hispanics. Familiar products such as plantains, mangoes, and other tropical fruits should also be on hand. The large retailer can also attract Hispanic customers if the store provides services that customers feel are important, especially working with the community on fund-raising or other events and providing an atmosphere for family shopping.

❙❙❙ ASIAN CUSTOMERS

The Asian-American market is small, only about 3 percent of the total population in 1990, or 7.6 million people. Still, the power of the Asian-American market is strong in certain areas. And the number of Asians in the U.S. is growing. By 2000, the Asian and Pacific Islander population could increase by almost 60 percent, to 12.1 million, according to Census Bureau projections.

The Asian population in America is growing in part because of immigration. In 1991, 3.5 percent of immigrants came from the Philippines, 3.0 percent came from Vietnam, and 1.5 percent hailed from Korea. Immigrants from mainland China accounted for 1.8 percent of the total that year, and Taiwanese accounted for 0.7 percent, according to the Immigration and Naturalization Service.

The states with the largest shares of Asians and Pacific Islanders are Hawaii (61.8 percent), California (9.6 percent), Washington (4.3 percent), New York (3.9 percent), Alaska (3.6 percent), New Jersey (3.5 percent), Nevada (3.2 percent), Maryland (2.9 percent), Virginia (2.6 percent), and Illinois (2.5 percent). Asians have made their presence felt in central cities and in suburbs. Suburban Asians tend to be more wealthy than their inner-city counterparts. These households had average incomes of $56,300 in 1991, while city Asians had incomes that were on average 25 percent lower.

Like Hispanics, it is impossible to consider Asians as one target market. Asians can be of Japanese, Chinese, Korean, Vietnamese, Filipino, or Laotian extraction. They may be American-born and assimilated, or they may be immigrants who have settled in enclaves with others from their own country. Unlike Hispanics, who are joined by a common language, Asians have dozens of different mother tongues. Even among Asians from the same country, different dialects can make communication difficult.

Generally speaking, Asians are more wealthy than other minorities, but Asians can be rich or poor. Recent immigrants from Cambodia,

Laos, and other poorer Asian nations have especially low incomes. Some Asians are college-educated; others work hard to ensure that their children will be. Filipinos, Indians, and some other Asian groups have been exposed to English in their home countries and quickly mainstream into American culture. But others tend to remain in neighborhoods where they can shop, eat, work, and converse in their native tongue.

Asians to 2000

Asians are America's fastest-growing minority market.

(Asian population by age, in thousands, 1990 and 2000, and percent change 1990-2000)

age	1990	2000	% change 1990-2000
total	7,458	12,125	62.6%
less than 5	638	1,056	65.7
5 to 9	612	989	61.6
10 to 14	564	955	69.3
15 to 19	626	952	52.1
20 to 24	661	895	35.4
25 to 34	1,467	2,112	44.0
35 to 44	1,261	2,023	60.4
45 to 54	717	1,425	98.7
55 to 64	472	833	76.5
65 to 74	300	555	85.0
75 to 84	122	261	113.9
85 and older	29	69	137.9

Source: Bureau of the Census

I I ASIAN FOODS

Like Hispanics, Asians have a strong sense of community and family commitment. Families shop for food together, and older family members strongly influence the family's shopping decisions, says Ronald D. Michman, author of *Lifestyle Market Segmentation.* Unlike Hispanics, little research has been done on their specific shopping and spending

You Don't Have To Be Jewish

The Hebrew word "kosher" means "proper" or "fit." Food that is certified kosher must meet rigorous standards of Jewish law, which can vary widely depending on the nature of the product. There are some foods such as pork, that can never be kosher; others receive certification only if they are prepared and packaged in certain ways. Foods that are kosher are marked with a U or a K. The symbol indicates that the product has been certified by rabbinic inspectors.

Jews who do not necessarily follow kosher law choose kosher foods because of the promise of purity. But the kosher food market is bigger than the religion itself. Non-Jews, including Seventh-Day Adventists, Moslems, vegetarians, allergy sufferers, people concerned about food additives, and people who want only the best quality foods, can be heavy purchasers of kosher products.

The New York City-based Orthodox Union, the largest non-profit organization that grants kosher certification, estimates that the U.S. has 6.5 million kosher food buyers. Sales of all products bearing the kosher symbol topped $31 billion in 1992. It is no wonder that some of the nation's leading food manufacturers such as Procter & Gamble, H.J. Heinz, Pillsbury, Best Foods, Kraft, and Coca Cola, go to the extra trouble of having their products kosher certified.

And it is a lot of trouble. All foods, their components, and their derivatives are divided into four categories: meat, milk, parve (anything that is not meat or milk, including eggs, plants, and fin fish), and non-kosher (which includes mixtures of meat and dairy, and mixtures of meat and fish). Each category has separate rules that must be followed to ensure that the food is kosher according to the laws of Kashruth.

Pork and pork products, most birds, all shellfish, all insects, all grapes derived from products that have not been supervised by a rabbi, all hard cheese products derived from ingredients that have not been supervised by a rabbi, all animals that have not been slaughtered and prepared according to Jewish law, and products that require mixing meat and milk or meat and fish are intrinsically not kosher. In addition, foods must be processed and packaged according to strict rabbinic regulations. Some kosher ingredients can be rendered non-kosher because of the way in which they were prepared.

Traditional kosher food manufacturers such as Hebrew National (ConAgra), Manischewitz, Rockeach Foods, Empire Kosher Poultry, and Aron Streit are trying to re-tool themselves to gain the growing kosher market. These companies have served a small, but loyal, constituency comprised primarily of observant Jews whose favorites include gefilte fish, borscht, and matzo balls. But new kosher consumers are looking for much more. To meet the need for mainstream foods, Empire Kosher Poultry now sells kosher pizza and lunch meat. Empire's strategy has paid off. Between 1992 and 1993, its sales increased over 14 percent, according to Information Resources Inc. of Chicago.

Meanwhile, mainstream food producers are going kosher. Gerber now has kosher baby cereal, and Dannon Yogurt certifies some of its products. Kosher meats are especially popular because kosher animals are not raised with growth-stimulating hormones.

Analysts expect the kosher market to increase dramatically. Kosher hot dogs and lunch meats are gaining in popularity. Some shoppers will only buy fresh meat from a kosher butcher. Because strict regulations make it impractical for some mainstream supermarkets to sell fresh kosher meat, many now carry frozen kosher chicken, turkey, Cornish game hens, and other products.

■ ■ ■

patterns. The Consumer Expenditure Survey does not yet distinguish Asian Americans in its statistics, and market research firms, daunted in part by the multitude of languages, have not undertaken detailed studies.

Asian supermarkets are filled with fresh vegetables and fruits—staples of the Asian diet. Fresh fish, another important food for the Asian population, is also highlighted. In the supermarket in the Yaohan Plaza (Arlington Heights, Illinois), Japanese customers can buy fresh fish flown in from California and Japan. The store sells myriad varieties of tofu and produce. It also has foods sought after by Koreans, Chinese, and other Asian clientele.

Supermarkets in areas in which Asian populations are dense highlight produce and fish in almost equal proportions. They are also designed with wider aisles to accommodate large family shopping groups, and with lower shelves to make it easier for smaller-framed Asians to reach products.

Although they are less likely than average to do so, more than half of Asian-American households surveyed in Market Segment Research's *1994 MSR Ethnic Market Report* purchased cooking oil, ice cream, ketchup, and ready-to-eat cereals within the month prior to the survey. Asian Americans are also light purchasers of breath mints, instant breakfast drinks, powdered soups, and powdered drink mixes. Fewer than 10 percent of the households surveyed purchased these products within the past month, and fewer than 25 percent purchased all-purpose dry seasonings, canned vegetables, desserts, dry pasta, instant stuffing, pancake mix, pancake syrup, refrigerated desserts, salad dressing, soda crackers, spread cheese, diet soft drinks, and evaporated milk.

Understanding minority marketing can be especially challenging when the minority is itself one of diversity. Asians, like Hispanics, are not all one group, regardless of how they may be perceived by Westerners. The cultures of China, Japan, Korea, Viet Nam, Cambodia, and other Asian cultures have many linguistic, cultural, and religious differences.

There are, however, some similarities that marketers may find useful to understand when targeting Asians. Many Asian immigrants avoid eye contact, a gesture they consider aggressive. And although many Asians speak and understand English, newcomers rarely initiate a conversation with a person they consider to be in a position of authority. Touching people of the opposite sex may also be considered offensive by some groups.

❚❚❚ OTHER MINORITIES

"We're all minorities now," asserts Martha Farnsworth Riche, current director of the U.S. Bureau of the Census and former director of policy studies at the Population Reference Bureau in Washington, D.C. "If you count men and women as separate groups, all Americans are now members of at least one minority group," she says. Ethnic differences, religious preference, and racial backgrounds all distinguish the multicultural nature of this country.

Marketers are becoming more sensitive to the needs of different minorities. Targeting the needs of different consumer groups is one of the best ways to make consumers customers. Food marketers should understand and profit from the diverse constituents in the neighborhoods in which their stores are located. This is especially important when a chain store opens up in a minority area. Upper level managers should be sensitive to the needs of constituent groups who will frequent the new store. Know the preferences and shopping habits of minorities. Be sure to provide products—and brands—they prefer. And even though a large supermarket cannot recreate the feel of a neighborhood corner store, marketers should try as much as possible to let shoppers feel at home—with familiar signs, sounds, and smells.

Familiar faces are also important. Marketers should be sure to hire from within the community. They should also take advantage of community functions—softball leagues, scouting events, or environmental programs—to get their name known and to build store loyalty.

CHAPTER 7

Regional Trends

THE GROCERY shopper in Los Angeles is not the same as the New York City shopper. Nor is the person at the big-city supermarket the same as the shopper at the country store. Regional trends are as big an influence on food shoppers as are age or ethnicity.

But understanding regional differences can be challenging. The lines between regionality and demography blur easily. Is Southwestern cuisine Southwestern because of geography or because of the great number of Hispanics who live in that part of the country? Is consumption of soy products greater in California because it's "a west coast thing" or because of the large concentration of Asian Americans there?

Regional cuisine can be geographically driven, culturally driven, or even economically driven. Most likely, it is the result of all three influences. Take California cuisine, for example. This type of cooking celebrates the freshness and rich variety of California fruits and vegetables, a geographic influencer, but it also reflects the wide variety of people from different cultural backgrounds that live in the area. And it doesn't hurt to have a market willing to spend extra for something different.

Americans first learned about regional cuisine when they began to drive automobiles. Perhaps the best-known aficionado of regional recipes and regional food products was Duncan Hines, a name familiar to buyers of cake mixes and frosting-in-a-can. Unlike his female counterpart, Betty Crocker, the Kentucky-born restaurant and hotel critic Duncan Hines (1880–1958) was a real person. He gained fame throughout the 1930s and 1940s as an arbiter of good taste in all things related to food and travel. *Adventures in Good Eating, Duncan Hines' Vacation Guide,* and *Adventures in Good Cooking,* his guides to high-class eating and sleeping spots in the United States, Mexico, and Canada, made his name synonymous with excellence.

Duncan Hines entered the world of packaged foods in 1948, when he joined forces with Roy H. Park of Ithaca, New York. After they began marketing foods under the Hines-Park label, Hines continued to travel the country, preaching the benefits of good food and good eating. His newspaper column, "Adventures in Good Eating at Home," provided readers with a wealth of culinary resources. Hines could be counted on to ferret out even the most obscure recipe from his vast personal library of cook books. He also provided instructions so that home chefs could recreate some of the choicest menus from the nation's most exclusive restaurants.

A champion of the merits of regional cuisine long before the "trendy foods" of the 1990s made such regional standards as chili and bagels as American as hamburgers and steak, Hines' influence waned in the post-war years. Although the interstate highway system connected the nation from coast to coast, many of the quaint and authentic regional eateries that Hines discovered proved to be too far off the exit ramp for travelers to visit. Soon roadside dining became as generic as the highways themselves.

As the twentieth century draws to a close, skilled chefs and talented food writers have come to the rescue of regional cuisine. Perhaps the best known are Jane and Michael Stern, authors of a number of books, including *Roadfood,* a 1990s version of Hines' *Adventures in Good Eating.*

A renewed interest in regional cuisine has made it possible to buy Hawaiian mahi-mahi in New York and New York bagels in Los Angeles. And regional cooking is not just a restaurant phenomenon—it is catching on at home as well. Cooking magazines like *Gourmet* feature regional recipes, and numerous cook books on regional cuisines have been published in the last few years. The growing sophistication of American taste buds has raised many regional standards to the level of gourmet fare.

With modern shipping and handling, there is very little "seasonality" inside grocery stores. Tomatoes can be found year round almost everywhere. Even seasonal delicacies such as asparagus, strawberries, and blueberries are in the produce sections of stores throughout the country in February as well as in June. Even so, the availability of fresh foods is still a determining factor for many shoppers. Aficionados of

The Age of Regions

The South is the largest, the Northeast is the oldest, the West is the youngest, and the Midwest is definitely the middle.

(regional population by age, in thousands, 1992)

age	Northeast	Midwest	South	West
total	51,118	60,713	88,143	55,108
less than 5 years	3,702	4,493	6,633	4,684
5 to 9	3,387	4,441	6,305	4,216
10 to 14	3,272	4,488	6,312	4,028
15 to 19	3,172	4,169	6,077	3,655
20 to 24	3,767	4,468	6,696	4,119
25 to 34	8,481	9,735	14,553	9,693
35 to 44	8,013	9,391	13,602	8,897
45 to 54	5,706	6,487	9,494	5,730
55 to 64	4,495	5,077	7,315	4,041
65 to 75	4,047	4,433	6,451	3,528
75 to 84	2,344	2,647	3,635	1,940
85 and older	734	881	1,070	574
median age	34.8	33.6	33.4	32.2

Source: Bureau of the Census

fresh foods maintain that a January tomato grown in a hothouse is tasteless and too expensive, and that strawberries imported from California in March just don't measure up to the ones grown locally in June. Other regional fare, such as Omaha steaks, Santa Fe salsa, and Hawaiian macadamia nuts do well regardless of the season.

The migration of populations from state to state have contributed to the changing product mix in supermarkets. Take the case of the roving blueberry. Northeasterners are very fond of their blueberries—in fact New Jersey is the largest exporter of fresh unprocessed blueberries in the country. But when Northeasterners retired to Florida, they were shocked to find that fresh blueberries were not readily available. Floridians, although well-versed in more tropical fruits, were not big consumers of that northern delicacy.

"We had a really difficult time selling fresh blueberries in the South," says Dennis Doyle, general manager of the Tru-Blu Cooperative Association in Lisbon, New Jersey. "People just didn't know what to do with them." But with a little pressure from the transplanted Northerners, and some aggressive marketing by New Jersey blueberry cooperatives, blueberries are now found in almost every supermarket that serves Florida retirement communities.

I I ■ FROM NORTH TO SOUTH

Distinguishing between the spending patterns of Northeasterners and Westerners or Midwesterners and Southerners is more complicated than simply comparing numbers. Food prices vary nationwide—especially prices for fresh produce. California oranges are usually less expensive in Los Angeles than they are in Duluth. Prices also vary on a seasonal basis. Fresh cherries are much more expensive in New York City at the end of February than they are in June when they can be bought locally.

Household size also plays an important role in regional food spending. In the Northeast, the average household or consumer unit* contains 2.4 people, according to the Bureau of Labor Statistics' 1992 Consumer Expenditure Survey. This figure is 2.5 in the South and 2.6

The Bureau of Labor Statistics' consumer units are not exactly comparable to households as defined by the Bureau of the Census.

in the Midwest. In the West the average household contains 2.7 people.

The typical American household spent about $2,600 for food at home in 1992. But Northeastern food shoppers spent more than those in other areas of the country on food at home—$2,800 per household in 1992, compared with a low of $2,500 in the South. And even on a per capita basis, Northeasterners spend more—about $1,180 per person annually, compared with $1,040 in the West, $990 in the South, and $980 in the Midwest.

Northeasterners spend more per capita on milk and cream, cereal and bakery products, beef, and poultry than people in other regions. Southerners spend the most on over-the-counter and prescription drugs. On a per capita basis, Southerners spend the least on milk and cream and cereal and bakery products. Midwesterners spend less on beef, poultry, and fresh fruits and vegetables. Westerners spend the least on prescription and over-the-counter drugs.

A number of factors contribute to regional differences in spending, among them age, ethnicity and race, taste, diet, and economics. A community of Asian Americans will spend more on rice than the

The Regional Market Basket

Consumers in the Northeast spend more than average on most things, with the exception of ground beef and potato chips.

(average household expenditures for selected grocery products, by region, 1992)

product	all consumers	Northeast	Midwest	South	West
Fresh fruit	$127.39	$143.77	$115.17	$111.87	$150.96
Milk and cream	133.81	140.79	134.86	125.00	139.73
Fresh vegetables	126.58	152.52	105.08	114.94	145.36
Poultry	123.10	170.29	103.85	114.73	111.86
Ground beef	86.66	82.30	92.88	86.64	83.51
Bread	76.28	87.04	75.70	69.38	77.22
Potato chips/nuts/snacks	75.64	70.91	80.42	68.85	85.77
Nonprescription drugs	74.51	77.03	67.17	79.80	72.28
Toilet paper/tissues	56.62	64.56	55.89	53.50	54.42
Coffee	38.95	44.50	36.96	35.88	40.71

Source: Bureau of Labor Statistics, 1992 Consumer Expenditure Survey

national average, while a community in which the majority of residents are Hispanic will spend more on beans than average. It is not surprising that even though Southerners have lower incomes on average, the region's large concentrations of older Americans drives up spending on over-the-counter and prescription drugs.

Prices for some products depend on the distance they must travel to market, and on the stages they go through on the way. If the farm-fresh product has to spend a few days in a refrigerated storage warehouse, it will increase in price.On the other hand, if a product can move to market quickly, it may be less expensive. Beef may be cheaper in the Midwest in part because it is so readily available.

Three major factors influence food prices: the farm value of food, the cost of processing and distributing it, and consumer demand. The last two are directly affected by the general economy. Slow growth during the early part of the 1990s contributed to slow increases in the price of food.

The farm value of food is the cost of farm commodities used in finished food products. It accounts for about 30 percent of retail costs. The farm value for a number of food categories decreased in 1993, but cold and wet weather throughout the first half of 1993 caused higher farm prices for red meats and vegetables, according to Ralph L. Parlett, an agricultural economist with the USDA's Economic Research Service. Higher farm prices led to an overall 2 percent increase in price for food at home that year.

❘❙❘ "QUILT CUISINE"

"Quilt cuisine" is a term coined to describe one of the latest food fads sweeping the country. *The Food Channel* says it's "more homespun than cross-cultural, less trend oriented or upscale than 'fusion,' and representing the sum total of American cooking today." The philosophy of quilt cooking involves all American cultures and their food—including more than 60 countries and over 500 years of immigration and integration.

Depending on indigenous foods and immigration patterns, quilt cuisine means different things in different parts of the country. Traditions and ingredients become transposed, and new hybrid styles of

Comfort Food

Comfort foods are foods that make you feel good when things are really bad—or make you feel even better when things are really good. But these emotion-inducing foods are different for people in different parts of the country. To New Englanders, it may be a big bowl of clam chowder, while Midwesterners may take comfort in a bowl of cream of tomato soup and soda crackers.

Some people crave meat loaf and mashed potatoes, just like Mom used to make. But even comfort standards vary from region to region. Should the potatoes be smooth or lumpy? Are they flavored with garlic or laced with melted cheese? Does the meat loaf have pork or beef in it? Is it spiced with cilantro, cumin, or good old ketchup? It all depends on where you live.

Comfort foods can fill the void in many different situations. When people are sick, they turn to soup, juice, tea, toast, and ice cream, according to a 1993 *Parade* magazine survey. But when they are depressed, they are more apt to eat chocolate, cookies, ice cream, or pizza.

Women are more likely than men to turn to chocolate (43 percent versus 27 percent). They are also more likely to find solace in a box of cookies (39 percent versus 27 percent). But men on a downer are more likely than women to eat ice cream (32 percent versus 30 percent) or soup (22 percent versus 13 percent).

When they are sad, happy, or just plain bored, 42 percent of men and 49 percent of women go on food binges. Women are twice as likely as men to binge when they are down (42 percent versus 21 percent). But men are more likely to use any excuse for a food binge. Sixty-nine percent of men said they binged when they were either happy or sad, as compared with 49 percent of women.

Supermarketers should know what to have on hand for the February blues, April tax time, or summer fun. Fifty-one percent of men and 56 percent of women turn to potato chips first on a binge. Other popular binge outlets are cookies, chocolate bars, other sweets, and ice cream. But you'd better check which flavor is most popular in your area before stocking up!

cooking and eating emerge. Chic restaurants in California combine Asian and Italian influences to produce a completely new style of cooking. A recipe in a June 1994 issue of *Gourmet* magazine proposed a "tasty takeoff on Tuscany's classic *bruschetta*," made with store-bought tortillas, red onions, and Parmesan cheese. The same issue suggests making cole slaw with Indian-inspired popped mustard seeds and Italian risotto with quinoa, a grain first cultivated by the Incas.

The influence of Native American foods and cooking styles is most prevalent in the Pacific Northwest, an area also influenced by Chinese and Japanese immigrants. Asian and Pacific Islanders have brought their own foods and cooking styles to California, an area also inhabited by Hispanics. The Mexican flavor of Texas foods is well known, but nearby Louisiana has other influences—including French, Cajun, and Creole.

Latin America and Africa (often by way of the Caribbean) have shaped many of the eating habits of Floridians and other Southeastern-

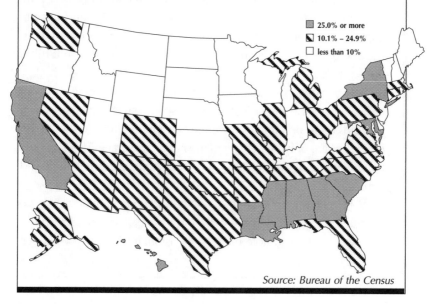

States of Racial Mix

States with the lowest shares of nonwhite population are mostly in the Midwest, and states with highest shares of minorities are mostly in the South.

(percent of state population, that is nonwhite, 1990)

■ 25.0% or more
■ 10.1% – 24.9%
□ less than 10%

Source: Bureau of the Census

Texas Tastes
▓ ▓ ▓ ▓ ▓ ▓ ▓ ▓ ▓ ▓ ▓ ▓ ▓ ▓

There are regions and then there is Texas. What is it about that state that sets it apart? Is it the vast, open spaces? The frontier spirit? The climate?

Researchers point to Texas' unique demographic profile. Texas has one of the highest proportions of Hispanic families in the nation. A large share of its population are children and teens, and a small share are aged 55 and older. Texans are more likely than other Americans to have large families, and there are more children in the average Texas home than in the average American family.

And then there is the question of Texas style. The clichéd image of a well-turned-out Texas woman—complete with immaculate hair, make-up, carefully chosen clothes, and accessories to match—is backed up by consumer data. Texans spend more on hair spray than the average American. They also spend more on cosmetics, deodorant, and diet pills, according to data gathered by the Chicago-based Information Resources, Incorporated (IRI). Texas style translates into food choices as well—with a heavy Hispanic accent. Supermarkets throughout the state stock a wide array of salsa, chilies, and other Latino favorites. Some stores even boast fresh tortillas baked daily.

Texans don't consume as much butter as other Americans—an indication of the pervasiveness of Hispanic-style cooking, which depends more on oil than butter. In San Antonio and Austin, butter purchases are only 36 percent of the national average. They are only half the national average in Dallas/Fort Worth, according to the IRI figures.

With its large population of babies and young children, it is no wonder that Texas leads the nation in the purchase of baby foods, formulas, and disposable diapers. Houstonians bought 44 percent more formula and 43 percent more disposable diapers than the national average in 1993.

The fastest-growing product categories in Texas supermarkets include iced-tea drinks, refrigerated prepared salads and cole slaws, liquid diet supplements, refrigerated tortillas, and fresh bagels. Granted, these products are also selling well in supermarkets throughout the country, but they are REALLY hot in Texas. Iced-tea drinks increased a whopping 2,350 percent in a three-month period between April and July of 1993 in Dallas/Forth Worth. During the same time, sales of iced-tea drinks increased 863 percent in Houston and 537 percent in San Antonio, compared with 191 percent in the country in general.

As for bagels—that's a different story. Bagels originated in eastern Europe, and were brought to America with the tens of thousands of Jewish immigrants, most of whom entered the country at Ellis Island in the late 19th century. As Jews traveled westward, so did bagels, and as Jews assimilated into American culture, so did bagels. It is not unusual to find bagels in flavors ranging from blueberry to pizza—a great change from the plain bagels of the past century.

And it is their variety that has boosted the bagel's acceptance among non-Jewish consumers. Texans, for example, only became aficionados of the bread product during the past few years, when the variety of flavors increased enough to capture their attention.

Bagels in Texas, salsa in Maine—regionality has taken on a new appearance as Americans become more interested in trying the foods from other parts of the country. Duncan Hines would be proud.

ers. In the Northeast, however, European foods and cooking styles share supermarket space with Middle Eastern and South American products. The Midwest is still strongly influenced by European foods, but the increased presence of Asian immigrants is beginning to introduce different ingredients into their recipes.

While some food forecasters predict that American cuisine will become even more hybridized as trends move up and down the map, there are still some regional tastes that do not migrate as easily as others. Even with the increased interest in American regional cooking, it is unlikely that Louisiana alligator will become a staple of the meat department in supermarkets in Minnesota or that amaranth, an Aztec grain, will replace rice in mainstream recipes.

▮▮ REGIONAL FOODS, NATIONAL TASTES

During the 1980s, yuppies were always looking for something new and different. At the same time, America's minorities were asserting themselves as distinct cultures. Immigrants jumped into the American melting pot, but they brought their own recipes. Some regional and ethnic foods caught on fast. Today, the favorite condiment is salsa and tortilla chips are the second-most popular snack behind potato chips.

Hispanic and Tex-Mex foods have become so popular that just about every major food manufacturer has at least one Hispanic-influenced product on the shelves. But the preferred type of salsa, green or red, mild or spicy, varies from region to region. Surprisingly, the spiciest prepared salsas aren't that popular in Texas, the home of Tex-Mex cuisine. Pace Foods Company of San Antonio reports that more of its hottest salsa is sold in Minnesota than in Texas.

"What makes a good egg roll in Atlanta may not go over in Des Moines," said Mark Willes, vice chairman of General Mills, in a 1993 interview. The big food conglomerate adjusts the menus at its Red Lobster, Olive Garden, and China Coast chains of restaurants to suit local palates. Lasagna served at the Olive Garden in Syracuse, New York is spiced and sauced to suit the taste of Central New Yorkers. The same dish tastes different in Los Angeles, Houston, and Kansas City.

And it is not just restaurant food that is being modified to suit regional palates. That ubiquitous can of Campbell Tomato Soup is not the same in every store in every part of the country. Instead, there are variations in flavor and spice levels designed to appeal to people in different regions of the country.

Regionality gives a product a certain cachet. Manufacturers, especially small food processing companies, are cashing in on our interest in regional cuisine by marketing products that proclaim their product's state of origin. In 1991, 3 percent of the new products launched in food stores were christened with state or regional names, according to Lynn Dornblaser, publisher of *New Product News*. Among the most popular were products with "Texas," "Vermont," "Hawaii," or "California" in their names. Also common were products with "American," "Southwest," or "Dakota" on their labels.

Even though their names may reflect their Southwestern origins, salsas are made in every part of the country. Texas Best picante sauce is made by the T. Marzetti Company of Columbus, Ohio. Old El Paso salsa hails from St. Louis, Missouri. Texas Pete hot sauces are made by T. W. Garner Foods in Winston-Salem, North Carolina.

But the manufacturers of "real" Texas salsa are beginning to fight back. The Pace Foods Company of San Antonio recently launched a television ad campaign in which salsas made in New York City—and the people who bought such products—were vilified. Instead, the ads maintain, people should only eat "authentic" salsas—those made in Texas.

I I ■ ORGANIC FOODS AND REGIONALITY

In 1962, Euell Gibbons introduced Americans to the concept of natural foods with his best-seller *Stalking the Wild Asparagus*. It was the perfect time to launch an assault against the processed, chemical-laden foods of the "older generation." That same year, Rachel Carson published her exposé of the food pesticide industry, *Silent Spring*. Almost overnight, counter-cultural citizens had a new enemy to battle—the packaged-food industry.

In the 1960s, the biggest food fears revolved around MSG (monosodium glutamate) and cyclamates. MSG, a natural flavor enhancer extracted from seaweed, was commonly added to Chinese and other foods to give the taste a "kick." But researchers found that it also caused brain damage in baby mice. Soon MSG was dropped as an additive to baby foods. The group of synthetic sweeteners known as cyclamates were commonly used in diet sodas and processed low-calorie foods until the late 1960s, when researchers discovered that exceedingly high

Organic Is Better!

Most people think the natural forms of food products are better or the same as other forms of the product.

(percent of adults who think that natural forms of selected food items are better, the same, or not as good as other forms of the item, by region, 1993)

item	Northeast	Midwest	South	West
Organically grown fruits/vegetables				
Better	53%	49%	50%	61%
Same	27	20	25	18
Not as good	5	7	9	6
Don't know	15	23	17	16
Natural cereal				
Better	45	46	45	55
Same	38	36	31	24
Not as good	6	5	9	9
Don't know	11	14	15	13
Free range chicken				
Better	38	44	46	41
Same	32	25	26	24
Not as good	5	2	8	8
Don't know	25	29	20	27
Free range eggs				
Better	36	39	40	40
Same	31	25	29	28
Not as good	5	4	9	7
Don't know	28	31	22	25
Natural soft drinks				
Better	30	26	28	33
Same	40	39	36	32
Not as good	13	11	15	11
Don't know	17	24	21	24

Note: Numbers do not add to 100 percent because of missing reponses.
Source: Roper Starch Worldwide, New York, NY

quantities of cyclamates caused cancer in laboratory rats. Soon cyclamates (but not saccharine) disappeared from the market.

Since the 1960s, food fears have encompassed myriad natural and artificial substances—Alar in apples, irradiated fruits and vegetables, milk from cows given bovine growth hormones, DDT, salmonella in chickens and melons. Headlines defending or condemning various food products have been appearing with frightening rapidity. Food safety is an important issue for all shoppers, but shoppers who want organic foods are much more likely than anyone else to be extremely concerned about chemical residues in produce and grains, antibiotics and hormones in meat and poultry, and pollution in fish and seafood.

After the 1989 Alar scare, shoppers began seeking out organic foods more actively, according HealthFocus, Incorporated of Des Moines. Publicity about the danger to children's health from pesticides used on farm crops pushed many shoppers to try organic foods for the first time. In a 1990 survey, 39 percent of U.S. shoppers said that they used organic produce, grains, or prepared foods. In 1992, about 30 percent of shoppers said that they used organic foods. The numbers may have decreased in part because the media found other "food fears" on which to focus—cholesterol, fat, and other health and lifestyle issues.

HealthFocus' 1992 survey showed that people in different parts of the country have embraced the organic food trend to varying degrees. New England shoppers have the greatest preference for organic foods—41 percent of people from that part of the country are likely to use organic products. Following closely behind are residents of the Pacific and Mountain regions (36 percent each) and Mid-Atlantic residents (almost 31 percent) followed by 29 percent of South Atlantic and North Central residents. People in the South Central states are the least likely to "go natural"—24 percent use organic foods. Suburban residents are the most likely to use organic foods (33 percent), followed closely by urban residents (32 percent), versus 30 percent of people living in small towns and 25 percent of rural shoppers.

Many foods are labeled "organic" or "all natural," but are they really what they claim to be? To help the consumer decide, the federal government is setting standards for the production, processing, and certification of organic foods. The Organic Food Production Act of

1990, under the supervision of the U.S. Department of Agriculture, has established a National Organic Standards Board charged with developing the guidelines for certifying foods to be organic. The act, which was implemented in 1994, regulates all crops, meat, dairy, and processed foods. If a product is not "all natural" it must now specify which components are organic. For example, a blueberry muffin mix made with organic blueberries can no longer be labeled "organic blueberry muffin mix." Instead, it will have to say "muffin mix made with organic blueberries." Organic farms must replenish their soil without using synthetic pesticides or fertilizers. And organic products must be minimally processed, without artificial ingredients, preservatives, or irradiation to maintain the integrity of the food.

Shoppers have become very conscious about food additives and food safety, and their awareness is increasing almost daily. But this awareness is not necessarily reflected in purchasing patterns. According to a 1993 Roper Starch Worldwide Study, while 53 percent of Americans thought that organically grown fruits and vegetables were better than those grown in the normal way, only 19 percent actually bought the organic variety in the past year. And while 43 percent of Americans acknowledged that free range chickens—birds allowed to roam freely and avoid chemically enhanced feed—had an advantage over fowl raised in the standard manner, only 6 percent purchased free range chickens.

Americans do believe in natural cereal, however. According to Roper, 47 percent feel that natural cereals are better than the usual run-of-the-mill products, and 30 percent bought a natural cereal in the past year.

Buying foods that are natural or organic gives consumers the feeling that they are taking care of themselves. Organic food users are twice as likely as other shoppers to agree strongly that their diet is very important to them—29 percent versus 15 percent, according to the HealthFocus study. Organic food users are also highly committed to watching what they eat. They are 75 percent more likely than those who don't use organic foods to agree strongly that they think about the nutritional value or healthfulness of the foods they eat—35 percent versus 20 percent.

Organic shoppers are much more apt than those who don't shop organic to say that they are knowledgeable about health and nutrition issues. They are also eager to share information on nutrition and health among their circle of friends. Forty percent of organic food users report that their friends asked them for nutritional advice, compared with 20 percent of those who don't use organic foods. Making nutritional information available to food shoppers may be one way to integrate organic foods into the mainstream food store. Many supermarkets are making organic produce more readily available, and some have expanded their shelf space to incorporate organic dry groceries, health and beauty aids, and other products.

Organic food shoppers are highly educated. College graduates and those with higher degrees are much more likely to use organic foods than people who are less educated. Thirty-six percent of organic food users are college graduates, compared with 13 percent of the adult population in general. But there is no significant difference when looking at affluence. Shoppers with average annual incomes below $25,000 are just as likely to use organic foods as those earning more.

Single shoppers are more likely than either married couples or unmarried partners to buy organic foods. Thirty-five percent of singles buy organic, compared with almost 28 percent of shoppers who are married or living with someone. Thirty-four percent of one-person households use organic foods, compared with 31 percent of two- or three-person households and 28 percent of larger households.

Surprisingly, families with children are less likely to use organics than those without children. Even though the press has devoted much of its coverage of organic food issues to children's health, 28 percent of families with children use organic food, compared with almost 34 percent of families that are child-free.

In the early days, organic foods and other "natural" products, from vitamins to health and beauty aids and homeopathic remedies, were usually sold in small, cooperatively-run stores. With the proliferation of supermarket-style chain stores, the natural product industry has grown to a 5-billion-dollar-a-year business, according to the *Natural Foods Merchandiser*. About 5 percent of natural products stores in 1993 were "natural products supermarkets" that sold everything from food to home remedies and food processing equipment.

Although New Englanders express the greatest preference for organic foods, the biggest dollar share of the organic market is in the Pacific. Forty-one percent of total spending in natural food stores occurred in the Pacific states (Alaska, Hawaii, California, Oregon, and Washington), even though those states are home to only 16 percent of Americans. According to Boulder-based New Hope Communications' 1992 Market Overview, that's about $1.5 billion. The next biggest market is in the Northeast—Vermont, Maine, New Hampshire, New York, Rhode Island, Massachusetts, Connecticut, New Jersey, and Pennsylvania. These states are home to 20 percent of all Americans, and they accounted for 15 percent of spending in these specialty stores in 1992, or about $535 million.

While the Mountain states (Montana, Idaho, Wyoming, Utah, and Colorado) are home to 3 percent of Americans, they make up 6 percent of the market, $215 million. The Midwest (Wisconsin, Michigan, Iowa, Missouri, Illinois, Indiana, and Ohio) is home to about 18 percent of all Americans, and accounted for almost 12 percent of total sales of natural food stores, about $430 million. The Eastern states (Kentucky, West Virginia, Virginia, Delaware, Maryland, Washington, D.C., North Carolina, South Carolina, and Tennessee) are home to 13 percent of Americans, and accounted for 8 percent of sales, $280 million. The Southeast (Arkansas, Mississippi, Alabama, Georgia, Louisiana, and Florida) had 13 percent of Americans, and 9 percent of sales, $305 million. The Southwest (Arizona, Nevada, New Mexico, and Texas) had 10 percent of the population and 7 percent of sales, $251 million. Finally, the Central states (North Dakota, South Dakota, Minnesota, Nebraska, Kansas, and Oklahoma) accounted for the smallest segment of the natural food pie. While they are 5 percent of all Americans, they made up less than 3 percent of 1992 sales, $101 million.

❙❚❙ SNACK FOOD GEOGRAPHY

When you think of junk food, do you instantly crave a bag of pretzels? You must be from one of the mid-Atlantic states. If a sack of pork rinds is your idea of heaven, you are most likely to be from the South. But if you are like really, really into multigrain chips, you are definitely from the West.

With sales of nearly $14 billion in 1992, the American snack-food industry is strongly affected by regional tastes and preferences. In 1992, Americans consumed some 5.2 billion pounds of snack foods, according to the *1993 Snack Food Association State-of-the-Industry Report.* The biggest overall snackers live in the West Central part of the country, where the per capita intake was nearly 24 pounds, and in the East Central region, where the average person consumed about 23 pounds. The most restrained snackers live in the Pacific and Southeast. In both regions less than 19 pounds per person is eaten annually.

If it is true that we are what we eat, then America is a nation of potato chips. The average American eats nearly 7 pounds of potato chips

The King of Snack Foods

Potato chips are number one for snacking, especially in the East Central areas, where annual consumption is 8.57 pounds per person.

(snack consumption of selected foods, in pounds per person, by region, 1992)

snack	New England	Mid Atlantic	East Central	Southeast
Potato chips	7.00	5.76	8.57	6.45
Tortilla chips	3.16	2.57	4.02	3.05
Microwave popcorn	1.76	1.36	1.61	1.36
Pretzels	1.97	3.97	2.62	1.34
Snack nuts	2.10	1.79	1.27	1.76
Pork rinds	0.01	0.04	0.13	0.29

snack	Southwest	West Central	Pacific
Potato chips	6.46	7.81	5.09
Tortilla chips	5.87	5.29	5.42
Microwave popcorn	1.06	1.48	1.18
Pretzels	0.87	1.79	1.03
Snack nuts	1.09	1.55	1.56
Pork rinds	0.33	0.12	0.18

Source: Snack Food Association, State of the Industry Report, 1993

annually. The heartiest potato-chip eaters live in the east central part of the country, where consumers typically eat almost 9 pounds of chips each year. And chips were the snack of choice in every part of the country except the Pacific region, where they were edged out by tortilla chips. On average, Pacific-coast snackers ate 5.1 pounds of potato chips in 1992, compared with 5.4 pounds of tortilla chips.

Tortilla chips are most favored by Southwesterners, who eat 6 pounds per capita each year. Snackers of the mid-Atlantic region were not nearly as enamored of tortilla chips. They consume less than 3 pounds per person annually. They are saving themselves for pretzels, which they consume at the rate of about 4 pounds per person per year—about four-and-a-half times more than Southwesterners. Touted as a low-fat snack, pretzels are beginning to gain in popularity in other parts of the country, but their primary market remains the Northeast.

Regionality is, to an extent, tied to ethnicity. Preferences in snack foods reflect certain food heritages that permeate different areas of the country. People in the Southwest, with its large Hispanic population, consume not only more tortilla chips than people in any other part of the country, but also more corn chips—almost 2 pounds per person, compared with the national average of less than 1 pound. Both snacks are made essentially from corn, a staple of Mexican, Tex-Mex, and Native American diets. Pretzels, which are favored in the "Northeastern Pretzel Belt" from the mid-Atlantic states into New England, reflect the snack food heritage of Germany, Austria, and other central European countries.

And regionality is also defined by tradition. Pork rinds are definitely a southern snack. Despite free advertising from former President George Bush, they have made little headway in other markets. Southwesterners consume about one-third of a pound, twice as much as Americans in general, and Southeasterners come in a close second. New Englanders eat the most popcorn and the most snack nuts. And people in the West Central part of the country eat the most meat snacks and the most party mix. Perhaps when marketing snack food, the adage should be changed to "You are where you eat."

APPENDIX

But How Do You Know What's Happening at Your Local Supermarket?

WHILE nationwide trends and shopping patterns are an excellent way for retailers to get a general sense of the current status of food shoppers across the country, they are by no means the whole picture. Of equal importance to retailers—whether they are independents or chains—is what is happening at the local level.

Retailers need to know whether their market areas are growing or declining, aging, and becoming more ethnically diverse. They need to know this for the county, city, suburb, and even the few blocks that surround their stores. Micro-regionality—the socioeconomic and cultural transformations, population movement, and even attitudes of shoppers in the local area that surrounds a grocery store—is of greater importance to a successful food retailer than those changes on a nationwide or even state basis.

There are a number of sources on which retailers can rely for local-area demographic information. Many federal agencies produce small-area statistics, but these data may be several years out of date by the time they become available. For more timely data, it is usually better to rely on local sources.

While local sources may have the information you want, that information may still be difficult to find. According to Judith Waldrop, research editor of *American Demographics* magazine, "the variety of local sources can be overwhelming." She suggests a number of ways to navigate the bureaucracy associated with them.

If a retailer is interested in several localities in one state, Waldrop suggests calling the state data center's lead agencies. These agencies have access to Bureau of the Census data, as well as those from more recent surveys. State data centers also produce estimates and projections of counties and other geographic areas within their respective states. They may also disseminate data compiled by other state agencies—departments of health, vital statistics, and education, to name a few.

But retailers must also look at an even smaller picture to get a feel for the demographic mix in the area in which their stores are sited. At the local level, city and county planning departments are a good place to look for demographic data. They may also be the source for local population and employment forecasts, both of which impact a food store's client composition.

Other city or county departments that collect demographic data include building departments, housing authorities, health departments, employment offices, boards of realtors, industrial and downtown development boards, and school boards.

Retailers looking for county or local-level data do not have to rely solely on government figures, however. Many nonprofit agencies and private companies generate local area projections. Nonprofit agencies, like the government, can provide data about the local population situation for free, or for a nominal charge. However, obtaining figures from a private company may cost hundreds or even thousands of dollars.

The Bureau of the Census and commercial data providers may not be able to produce local projections as accurate as those produced by the county or city government agencies for whom the data is more accessible and more pertinent. In many instances, local agencies are more up-to-date on the changes that affect a small area of a community. They know the parts of the community in which new development is bringing in younger families with children; they can predict the local impact of a new employer moving in or an established employer moving out. They can also monitor more closely the economic and demographic changes that are taking place and tabulate those data in a more timely manner than large government or commercial agencies.

There may be other sources of information in your community. You may be able to check with local newspapers whose research departments keep track of demographic trends in their circulation areas. Such newspapers may have research departments that are willing to share information with others.

But not all data can be distilled to the local level. Many surveys concerning health, shopping patterns, and food preferences are carried out by companies using demographically representative samples of the country as a whole. Interpreting these types of data on a local level may prove to be difficult. Sometimes, retailers may have to gather their own data by a somewhat unscientific method—by simply observing shoppers and seeing what they buy and how and when they buy it. Another method of tracking customer preferences is simply to ask them what they want—through store-wide surveys or questionnaires that shoppers can fill in when they visit the store.

❙❙❙ HOW TO FIND OUT MORE

For more information about how to get information, retailers may want to contact local and state government officials. To locate the state data center nearest you, call the Bureau of the Census' State Data Center Program at (301) 763-1580. For a comprehensive listing of state data centers and other state government agencies, see *The Insider's Guide to Demographic Know-How* by Diane Crispell, executive editor of *American Demographics*. The book, which also lists federal government agencies and private data companies, is updated regularly, and is available from American Demographics Books of Ithaca, New York; telephone (800) 828-1133.

References

CHAPTER 1

Ambry, Margaret, and Cheryl Russell. *The Official Guide to the American Marketplace*. Ithaca, New York: New Strategist Publications, 1992.

Bowman, Russell. *Couponing and Rebates, Profit on the Dotted Line*. New York: Lebhar Friedman Books, 1980.

Cross, Jennifer. *The Supermarket Trap: The Consumer and the Food Industry*. Bloomington, IN: Indiana University Press, 1970.

Dornblaser, Lynn. "New Product Review," Editors' Briefing Program. Food Marketing Institute 1994 Supermarket Industry Convention.

Dunn, William. "Fighting the Coupon Wars," *Marketing Tools,* April/May 1994, 59–60.

Elliott, Stuart. "Giant marketers up the ante in their coupon promotions, a nickel at a time," *New York Times,* September 2, 1993, D19.

"58th Annual Report of the Supermarket Industry," *Progressive Grocer,* April 1991, 58.

Food Institute Information and Research Center. *Food Retailing Review,* 1994 Edition. Fair Lawn, NJ: Food Institute Information and Research Center, 1994.

Food Marketing Institute. *Trends in the United States: Consumer Attitudes and the Supermarket, 1994*. Washington, D.C.: Food Marketing Institute, 1994.

"Groceries by remote control," *USA Weekend*, March 18–20, 1994, 18.

Kanner, Bernice. "Savings Plan," *New York*, September 7, 1992, 18–21.

Lebergott, Stanley. *Pursuing Happiness: American Consumers in the Twentieth Century*. Princeton, N.J.: Princeton University Press, 1993.

Mason, Michael. "The Man Who Has a Beef With Your Diet," *Health*, May/June 1994, 53–58.

Parade Magazine. *What America Eats, Volume IV*. 1993.

"61st Annual Report of the Grocery Industry," *Progressive Grocer*, April 1994.

Stacey, Michelle, *Consumed: Why Americans Love, Hate, and Fear Food*, New York: Simon & Schuster, 1994.

Stern, Jane, and Michael Stern. *American Gourmet*. New York: HarperCollins Publishers, 1991.

CHAPTER 2

Ambry, Margaret, and Cheryl Russell. *The Official Guide to the American Marketplace*. Ithaca, New York: New Strategist Publications, 1992.

Bounds, Wendy. "Market Matures for a Children's Remedy," *Wall Street Journal,* July 26, 1993.

Brouillette Research, Inc. *The Service Advantage: How to Win and Influence Shoppers, 1992.* 1992.

Cole, Catherine A., and Siva K. Balasubramanian. "Age Difference in Consumers' Search for Information: Public Policy Implications," *Journal of Consumer Research* 20 (1993); 157–169.

Eisman, Regina. "Young at Heart," *Incentive*, April 1993, 33–38.

Food Marketing Institute. *Trends 92*. Washington, D.C.: Food Marketing Institute, 1992.

"46th Annual Consumer Expenditure Study," *Supermarket Business.* September 1993.

Hammonds-Smith, Maxine, Joan C. Courless, and F.N. Schwenk. "A Comparison of Income, Income Sources, and Expenditure of Older Adults by Educational Attainment," *Family Economics Review* Vol. 5, No. 4 (1992) 2–8.

Moschis, George P. "Gerontographics: A Scientific Approach to Analyzing and Targeting the Mature Market," *Journal of Consumer Marketing*, 10 (1993), 43–53.

———— and Anil Mathur, "How They're Acting Their Age," *Marketing Management* 2:2 (1993), 41–50.

Schwenk, F.N. "Women 65 Years or Older: A Comparison of Economic Well-Being by Living Arrangement," *Family Economics Review* 4:3 (1991), 2–8.

————. "Income and Expenditures of Older Widowed, Divorced, and Never-Married Women Who Live Alone," *Family Economics Review* 5:1 (1992), 2–8.

————. "Changes in the Economic Status of America's Elderly Population During the Last 50 Years," *Family Economics Review*, 6:1 (1993), 18–27.

"60th Annual Report of the Grocery Industry," *Progressive Grocer*, April 1993.

Slaughter, Ed. *Prevention Magazine and the Food Marketing Institute Survey of Public Concern Regarding Good Nutrition*. Princeton, N.J.: 1992.

Snack Food Association. *Consumer Snacking Behavior Report*. Alexandria, VA: Snack Food Association, 1992.

Speer, Tibbett L. "Older Consumers Follow Different Rules," *American Demographics*, February 1993, 21–23.

Spiller, Lisa D., and Richard A. Hamilton. "Senior Citizen Discount Programs: Which Seniors to Target and Why," *Journal of Consumer Marketing* 10 (1993), 42–51.

Waldrop, Judith. "Old Money," *American Demographics*, April 1992, 24–32.

_____ with Marcia Mogelonsky. *The Seasons of Business: The Marketer's Guide to Consumer Behavior*, Ithaca, New York: American Demographics Books, 1992.

Walker, Rita Scott, and Frankie N. Schwenk. "Income and Expenditure Patterns of Consumer Units with Reference Person Age 70 to 79 and 80 or Older." *Family Economics Review* 4:1 (1991), 8–13.

Zeithaml, Valarie A., and Mary C. Gilly. "Characteristics Affecting the Acceptance of Retailing Technologies: A Comparison of Elderly and Nonelderly Consumers." *Journal of Retailing* 63 (1987), 49–68.

CHAPTER 3

Ambry, Margaret, and Cheryl Russell. *The Official Guide to the American Marketplace*. Ithaca, New York: New Strategist Publications, 1992.

Balzer, Harry. "The Ultimate Cooking Appliance," *American Demographics*, July 1993, 40–44.

Deveny, Kathleen. "For Coffee's Big Three, A Gourmet-Brew Boom Proves Embarrassing Bust," *Wall Street Journal*, November 4, 1993.

_____, and Eben Shapiro. "Stingy When Selecting Grocery Basics, Consumers Still Splurge on Fancy Foods," *Wall Street Journal*, August 10, 1993.

Dornblaser, Lynn. "New Product Review." Editors' Briefing Program. Food Marketing Institute 1994 Supermarket Industry Convention.

Fee, Caroline. "Grey Poupon Family Adds New Member," Nabisco Foods Group Press Release, September 21, 1989.

Food Marketing Institute. *Trends in the United States: Consumer Attitudes and the Supermarket, 1993*. Washington, D.C.: Food Marketing Institute, 1993.

_____. *Eating in America: Perception and Reality*. Washington, D.C.: Food Marketing Institute, 1994.

German, Gene A., Gerard F. Hawkes, and Debra J. Perosio. *Supercenters: The Emerging Force in Food Retailing*. Ithaca, New York: Department of Agricultural Economics, Cornell University, 1993.

Kanner, Bernice. "When You're Haute, You're Hot." *New York*. January 27, 1986, 14–19.

Mogelonsky, Marcia. "Grey Poupon." *Encyclopedia of Consumer Brands*. Detroit, MI: St. James Press/Gale Research Inc, 1994.

Parade Magazine. *What America Eats, Volume IV*. 1993.

"Rolls-Royces Block Road for Grey Poupon." *Advertising Age*, March 18, 1991, 42.

Russell, Cheryl. *100 Predictions for the Baby Boom: The Next 50 Years*. New York: Plenum Press, 1987.

Scroggins, John. "Good-bye, June Cleaver, II." *The Food Channel*. March 21, 1994, 7.

Smith, Ann. "Grey Poupon Is Cutting the Mustard Three New Ways." Nabisco Foods Group Press Release, November 18, 1992.

Snack Food Association. *Consumer Snacking Behavior Report*. Alexandria, VA: Snack Food Association, 1992.

Zandl, Irma, and Richard Leonard. *Targeting the Trendsetting Consumer: How to Market Your Product or Service to Influential Buyers*. Homewood, IL: Business One Irwin, 1992.

CHAPTER 4

Ambry, Margaret. *The Official Guide to Household Spending*. Ithaca, New York: New Strategist Publications, 1993.

American Demographics. *American Spending*. Desk Reference Series, No. 5, 1993.

Brouillette Research, Inc. *The Service Advantage: How Customers Evaluate Service in Their Supermarkets*. Cincinnati, Ohio, 1991.

_____. *How to Win and Influence Shoppers, 1992*. Cincinnati, Ohio, 1992.

Carson, Patrick, and Julia Moulden. *Green Is Gold: Business Talking to Business about the Environmental Revolution* Toronto, ON: HarperCollins Inc., 1991.

Crispell, Diane. "Movers of Tomorrow," *American Demographics*, June 1993, 59.

Dunn, William. *The Baby Bust: A Generation Comes of Age*. Ithaca, NY: American Demographics Books, 1993.

"Food Spending by Female-Headed Households: Review of Previous Research," *Family Economics Review*, 6:1 (1993), 32–34.

Food Marketing Institute. *Trends in the United States: Consumer Attitudes and the Supermarket, 1992*. Washington, D.C.: Food Marketing Institute, 1992.

Giles, Jeff. "The Myth of Generation X," *Newsweek*, June 6, 1994, 62-72.

"Green Consumerism in the Supermarket." *Green MarketAlert*, September 1992, 7–8.

Herbig, Paul, William Koehler, and Ken Day. "Marketing to the Baby Bust Generation," *Journal of Consumer Marketing*, 10:1 (1993), 4–9.

Lino, Mark. "Income and Expenditure of Families with a Baby," *Family Economics Review*, 4:3 (1991), 9–15.

_____ and Geraldine Ray. "Young Husband-Wife Households with Children," *Family Economics Review*, 5:1 (1992), 9–16.

Lutz, Steven M., James R. Blaylock, and David M. Smallwood. "Household Characteristics Affect Food Choices," *Food Review*, May-August 1993, 12–18.

Mitchell, Susan. "How to Talk to Young Adults," *American Demographics*, April 1993, 50–54.

Price, Charlene. "Fast Food Chains Penetrate New Markets," *Food Review*, January-April 1993, 8–12.

Slaughter, Ed. *Prevention Magazine and the Food Marketing Institute Survey of Public Concern Regarding Good Nutrition.* (Princeton, N.J., March 1992).

Snack Food Association. *Consumer Snacking Behavior Report.* Alexandria, VA: Snack Food Association, 1992.

"Special Report: The Future of Households," *American Demographics* December 1993, 27–40.

"Supermarkets Strut Their Stuff," *Green MarketAlert*, November 1990, 3–4.

CHAPTER 5

Ambry, Margaret. *The Official Guide to Household Spending.* Ithaca, New York: New Strategist Publications, 1993.

American Frozen Foods Institute, *Who's in the Kitchen with Dinner? Survey Finds Children Can Eat Well on Their Own.* New York, NY: American Frozen Foods Institute, 1990.

Bounds, Wendy. "Mood Is Indigo for Many Food Marketers," *Wall Street Journal*, September 2, 1993.

"Convenience Foods and the Microwave," A Good Housekeeping Institute Report. Consumer Research Department, April 1989.

Carson, Patrick, and Julia Moulden. *Green Is Gold: Business Talking to Business about the Environmental Revolution*. Toronto, ON: HarperCollins Inc., 1991.

Deveny, Kathleen. "Cereal Firms Make a Pitch to Snackers," *Wall Street Journal*, July 1, 1993.

"Estimated Annual Expenditures on a Child by Husband-Wife Families," *Family Economics Review*, 6:3 (1993), 34–36.

"Estimated Annual Expenditures on a Child by Single-Parent Families," *Family Economics Review*, 6:3 (1993), 37.

Frazao, Elizabeth. "Female-Headed Households Spend Less on Food," *Food Review*, May-August 1993, 6–11.

Greenwald, John. "Will Teens Buy It?" *Time*, May 30, 1994, 50–52.

Guadagno, Mary Ann Noecker. "Economic Status of Two-Parent Families with Employed Teens and Young Adults," *Family Economics Review*, 4:4 (1991), 2–10.

_____. "Impact of Children's Employment on the Economic Status of Two-Parent Families," *Family Economics Review*, 5:4 (1992) 9–16.

Harris/Scholastic Research, *The Kellogg Children's Nutrition Survey*, 1989.

"The Kid Factor," *Green MarketAlert*, February 1992, 6–7.

Lewis, Gary and Harvey H. Hartman. *The Hartman Environmental Marketing Strategies and Research Report*, Long Beach, CA: The Hartman Group, 1993.

Lino, Mark. "Income and Expenditures of Families with a Baby," *Family Economic Review*, 4:2 (1991), 9–15.

_____. "Families with Children: Changes in Economic Status and Expenditures on Children Over Time," *Family Economics Review*, 6:1 (1993), 9–17.

McNeal, James U. "Growing Up in the Market, *American Demographics,* October 1992, 50.

_____ and Chyon-Hwa Yeh. "Born to Shop," *American Demographics,* June 1993, 34–39.

Rust, Langbourne. "Observations: How to Reach Children in Stores— Marketing Tactics Grounded in Observational Research," *Journal of Advertising Research* 33:6 (1993), 67–72.

Seventeen magazine, *Seventeen 1993 Food Survey.* May 1993.

Simmons, Jacqueline. "Sales of Gooey, Flavored Milks Are Healthy," *Wall Street Journal,* November 11, 1993.

Simmons Marketing Series. *The New American Family: Significant and Diversified Lifestyles.* Simmons Market Research Bureau, Inc., 1992.

"Special Report: The Future of Households," *American Demographics* December 1993, 27–40.

Stipp, Horst. "New Ways to Reach Children," *American Demographics,* August 1993, 50–56.

Underhill, Paco. "Kids in Stores," *American Demographics,* June 1994, 22–27.

Zinn, Laura. "Teens: Here Comes the Biggest Wave Yet," *Business Week,* April 11, 1994, 76–86.

CHAPTER 6

"African Americans: A Sense of Community," *Food Business,* January 6, 1992, 18.

Ambry, Margaret, and Cheryl Russell. *The Official Guide to the American Marketplace.* Ithaca, New York: New Strategist Publications, 1992.

Braus, Patricia. "What Does Hispanic Mean?" *American Demographics*, June 1993, 46–49, 58.

Brewer, Gregory. "Spike Speaks," *Incentive*, February 1993, 26–4.

Eating in America: Perception and Reality. Prevention magazine special report, 1994.

Frey, William H. and William P. O'Hare. " Vivan los Suburbios," *American Demographics*, April 1993, 30–37.

Gorman, Christine. "Milking a Fad," *Time*, May 17, 1993, 53.

Gray, Gary M. *Milk intolerance due to lactase deficiency.* National Institute of Arthritis, Diabetes, and Digestive and Kidney Diseases, November 1990.

Hwang, Suein L. "Kosher-Food Firms Dive into Mainstream," *Wall Street Journal*, April 1, 1993.

_____. "Makers of Remedies Breed a Cash Cow As They Publicize Lactose Intolerance," *Wall Street Journal*, April 20, 1993.

"In an Age of Fragmentation, Mainstreaming Is Out as the Rifleman Takes Over," *Promo: The International Magazine for Promotion Marketing*, January 1992, 12.

Kaufman, Carol J. and Sigfredo A. Hernandez. "The Role of the Bodega in a U.S. Puerto Rican Community," *Journal of Retailing*, 67:4 (1991), 375–396.

Market Segment Research, *1994 MSR Ethnic Market Report* (Coral Gables, FL: Market Segment Research Inc., 1994.

Michman, Ronald D. *Lifestyle Market Segmentation*. New York: Praeger Publishers 1991.

Morris, Eugene. "The Difference in Black and White," *American Demographics*, January 1993, 44–49.

Oliver, Joyce Anne. "To Reach Minorities, Try Busting Myths," *American Demographics*, April 1992, 14–15.

Otto, Alison. "Processors Target the New Majority," *Food Business*, January 6, 1992, 14–15.

Rabin, Steve. "How to Sell Across Cultures," *American Demographics*, March 1994, 56–57.

Reisner, Jeff. "America's Untapped $200 Billion Market," *Food Business*, May 7, 1990, 12–13.

Riche, Martha Farnsworth. "We're all Minorities Now," *American Demographics*, October 1991, 26–34.

Ryan, Nancy. "Marketing to African American Consumers," *Chicago Sunday Tribune*, June 9, 1991.

Slaughter, Ed. *Prevention Magazine and the Food Marketing Institute Survey of Public Concern Regarding Good Nutrition.* (Princeton, N.J., March 1992).

Swenson, Charles A. *Selling to a Segmented Market: The Lifestyle Approach.* New York: Quorum Books, 1990.

Waldrop, Judith. "The Newest Southerners," *American Demographics*, October 1993, 38–43.

Weyr, Thomas. *Hispanic U.S.A.: Breaking the Melting Pot*, New York: Harper and Row, 1988.

Winsberg, Morton. "Specific Hispanics," *American Demographics,* February 1994, 44–53.

CHAPTER 7

Deveny, Kathleen. "What Is a Texas Consumer, Anyway?" *Wall Street Journal*, September 22, 1993.

_____. "What's in a Name? A Lot, if It's 'Texas'," *Wall Street Journal*, November 24, 1993.

Edmondson, Brad. "Place Names That Sell," *American Demographics*, April 1992, 42–43.

Food Retailing Review, 1994 Edition. Fair Lawn, N.J.: The Food Institute, 1994.

Gourmet's America. Gourmet magazine, special issue, April 1993.

Hammel, Ruth. "States of Mind," *American Demographics*, April 1992, 40–43.

Hines, Duncan. *Duncan Hines' Food Odyssey*, New York: Thomas Y. Crowell Company, 1955.

Imming, Bernard J. *Produce Management and Operations*, second edition. Ithaca, NY: Cornell University Home Study Program, 1990.

Kanner, Bernice. "What's in Store for You," *Parade*, November 14, 1993, 8–10.

Mogelonsky, Marcia. "Duncan Hines," *Encyclopedia of Consumer Brands*. Detroit, MI: St. James Press/Gale Research, 1994.

_____. "The Geography of Snack Food," *American Demographics*, July 1994, 12–13.

Organic Produce and Farming: Raising the Issues for Growers and *Sellers*. Alexandria, VA: United Fresh Fruit and Vegetable Association, n.d.

The Organic Trend Report. Des Moines, IA: HealthFocus, Inc., 1993.

Parade magazine. *What America Eats*, Volume IV, 1993.

Schremp, Gerry. *Kitchen Culture: Fifty Years of Food Fads*. New York, NY: Pharos Books, 1991.

Schwartz, David M. "Duncan Hines: he made gastronomes out of motorists," *The Smithsonian*, November 1984, 87–97.

Snack Food Association. *Consumer Snacking Behavior Report*. Alexandria, VA: Snack Food Association, 1992.

"12th Annual Market Overview, 1992," *Natural Foods Merchandiser*, June 1993.

Index

AMERICAN DEMOGRAPHICS BOOKS

Targeting Transitions: *Marketing to Consumers During Life Changes*
Millions of Americans go through major life transitions each year, including getting married or remarried, becoming parents and grandparents, changing careers, getting divorced, moving, becoming caregivers, and retiring. Once you understand the characteristics of people in transition, you can begin to discover the marketing opportunities created by these events.

The American Forecaster Almanac: *1994 Business Edition*
A fascinating compendium tracking key trends in almost every aspect of American culture, this book covers technology, consumer goods, business, health, education, fashion, entertainment, travel, and leisure.

The Insider's Guide to Demographic Know-How: *Everything You Need to Find, Analyze, and Use Information about Your Customers*
Now in its third edition, this useful sourcebook covers federal, state, local, private, and international sources of demographic data. It directs you to the right source of information and explains how to ask for the numbers you need.

Health Care Consumers in the 1990s: *A Handbook of Trends, Techniques, and Information Sources for Health Care Executives*
This Handbook makes the connection between demographic realities and related health care issues. It will help you define your target market and carve out a niche that you can serve profitably and effectively.

The Baby Bust: *A Generation Comes of Age*
As a generation, busters are unique in their experiences, beliefs, politics, and preferences. This is the first statistical biography of this generation. It tells their story through demographics, opinion polls, expert analysis, anecdotes, and the indispensable comments and experiences of busters themselves.

Targeting Families: *Marketing To and Through the New Family*
Word-of-mouth product recommendations made from one family member to another are significantly more effective than those made between friends or colleagues. Learn how to get family members on your sales force and how to implement a "Full Family Marketing" approach that attracts youths, spouses, and seniors.

Capturing Customers: *How to Target the Hottest Markets of the '90s*
Find out how to combine demographics with geographic, psychographic, and media preference data, and how to use consumer information to identify opportunities in nearly every market niche.

Beyond Mind Games: *The Marketing Power of Psychographics*
The first book that details what psychographics is, where it came from, and how you can use it.

Selling The Story: *The Layman's Guide to Collecting and Communicating Demographic Information*
A handbook offering a crash course in demography and solid instruction in writing about numbers. Learn how to use numbers carefully, how to avoid misusing them, and how to bring cold numbers to life by relating them to real people.

The Seasons of Business: *The Marketer's Guide to Consumer Behavior*
Learn which demographic groups are the principle players and which consumer concerns are most pressing in each marketing season.

Desktop Marketing: *Lessons from America's Best*
Dozens of case studies show you how top corporations in all types of industries use today's technology to find tomorrow's customers.

About the Author

■■■■■■■■■■■■■■■■■■■■■

Photo by Ronna Mogelon

Marcia Mogelonsky is a contributing editor of *American Demographics* magazine, writing a monthly column on supermarket and shopping trends. Her articles have appeared in *The Food Channel, Modern Woman, Marketing Tools,* and *The Numbers News.* Dr. Mogelonsky has also contributed to the *Encyclopedia of Consumer Brands* and the *Encyclopedia of American Industry,* as well as a number of books on the supermarket industry.

Dr. Mogelonsky received her B.A. and M.A. degrees from McGill University in Montreal, Canada. She was granted a Ph.D. from Cornell University in Ithaca, New York. She has completed postdoctoral social sciences and humanities research.

Dr. Mogelonsky lives with her husband and two children in Ithaca, New York, where she pursues an active freelance writing and consulting career.